Social Skills:

~

Improve Self-Esteem and Nonverbal Communication by Managing Shyness and Social Anxiety for Happier Relationships.

Gain Self-Confidence, Public Speaking, Friendships & Change Your Life.

Ted Goleman

Table of Contents

Introduction

Working on social skills takes time. Some people are just fast at learning while others are not. The fast people are natural at making conversation. The more one is able to make easy and relatable conversation then he or she forms bonds with others. The better the conversation then, the better the relationship. The relationships could be family, work relationship or even friendship.

The purpose of social skills is to develop conversations. Conversation skills are learned and nurtured over time. For one to be a good converse, then he or she must master confidence. Confidence is all that leads to a conversation. One must take a chance at others if he or she wants to make conversation. Well talking to others might come naturally while to others not so much. They then have to put in some effort and ensure that the conversation goes on without any hitches. After one has taken a chance on others, then one should talk the other people

The basic essential of conversing with people is one's ability to listen to them. It is always a good thing to listen to any situation. It is a bad habit just to talk and talk without listening. The people who keep and keep talking without listening to others are very annoying and are mostly ignored. One should learn to converse while listening to others. The conversation should not be one-sided, that is to avoid boredom. It is essential to know the art of talking while listening. The book has clearly shown the steps one must take to be a better listener.

Excellent social skills allow you to present your best self to those around you. They can provide you with the confidence to succeed in all situations, and the ability to get to know the people you would like to become close to. From being able to identify your strengths to knowing exactly how to carry on a conversation, your social skills will provide you with deeper social connections. No matter who you are talking to, it is a considerable boost in confidence to be able to converse, socialize, and generally get to know another person. This connectivity is what makes you feel secure in yourself and your interactions.

While socialization is profound and essential, it can be difficult for some. Working up the courage to talk to another person can often be intimidating, especially when you are unsure of yourself. Many people struggle with their social skills, wishing that they were better at the skills that come naturally to some. With practice, the techniques in this guide are meant to build you up so that you feel comfortable and confident about socializing, no matter where you are or where you go. From working on your body language to discovering how to talk to new people, you will obtain a renewed sense of confidence in yourself.

Starting at the very beginning, you will learn about the skills that you already possess. By harnessing your strengths, your weaknesses will be easier to overcome. Instead of feeling ashamed that you have weaknesses, you will learn how to transform them into traits that will make socialization easier. If shyness is a burden in your life, you will learn how to combat it in ways that still allow you to feel comfortable while also appearing more extroverted. With a simple boost to your charisma from growing your self-esteem, you will feel capable enough to handle any social interaction that comes your way.

Chapter 1

How To Know, Evaluate And Enhance Your Skills To Improve Self-Esteem

I am pretty sure you have heard the concept of self-esteem numerous times. Someone might have high or low self-esteem based on his personal opinion of himself and his abilities. It is normal for people to be skeptical of their ability once a while. However, low self-esteem kills one's motivation and passion for trying things out.

If you look inward, you might be able to identify a few things that affect your self-esteem. It might be an unhealthy comparison, being bullied, having an unrealistic expectation of yourself, etc. One of the best things you can do to make your life have a positive turnaround is improving your self-esteem. With improved self-esteem and confidence in yourself and your ability will grow, which will also translate to improved social skills.

Why is Improving Your self esteem pretty important?

You Live a Simple and Happier Life
When you have a good and high opinion about yourself, you will be kinder to yourself. As a result, life becomes kinder, and simple mistakes will not drag you excessively. The understanding that you are not perfect has already sunk into you, hence you embrace mistakes.

10

You will live a Stable life

Having a high opinion of yourself, without being cocky, and your ability will prevent you from seeking validation from others. As a result, the rate at which you seek to please people decreases. This will reward you with inner stability since what people say about you will have very little effect.

You will Enjoy Your relationships More

Better self-esteem makes you comfortable with yourself. Your life becomes simpler as there will be less drama, less comparison, and more contentment over your life in general. This makes you enjoy all the relationships you have, be it a friend or a romantic partner.

There are many benefits that come from improving your self-esteem. However, that is not the theme of this chapter. Our main aim is to dish out practical steps you can take to improve your self-esteem.

Practical Ways to Improve Your Self Esteem

Always Have Realistic Expectations

One of the easiest ways to kill self-esteem is by having unrealistic expectations. Failure to achieve that expectation can make you feel inadequate, dealing a big blow on your self-esteem. I remembered when I received my acceptance letter into university. I told myself I must graduate with a first-class honor degree or else I am a failure. Anyway, the time of graduation came, and my grade was pretty far from first class. It marred my confidence and made me lose faith in myself. As expected, my self-esteem was shattered when my goal could not be achieved.

Doing away with unrealistic expectations could be the antidote you need to quit beating yourself up. When our expectations are realistic, we are confident that we will achieve our goals, which in turn won't affect the way we perceive ourselves.

Do Away With Perfections and Celebrate Your Accomplishments

One of the easiest ways to remain miserable is always striving for perfection. Yet, it is high time many of us come to terms with the fact that we will never be perfect. You will not get the perfect bikini body, the perfect girlfriend, the perfect vehicle, the perfect job, etc. All these are simply illusions that only exist in our mind.

Rather than tormenting yourself with some idealized sense of perfection, celebrate your accomplishments. As you reach each milestone, celebrate them, no matter how easy it was. You can get a journal to have a list of your accomplishments as they unfold. This is a tested way to believe in yourself and your ability.

Rather than aiming for perfection, you can settle for good enough. This is not a license to slack or not give tasks and projects your best. But perfection will make you critical; will end up hurting you and the people in your life.

Keep in mind that life is different from what you see in the movies. With this in mind, when your expectation is not so high, it will not be too shocking or devastating when reality sets in.

Ditch the Comparison Game

One of the easiest ways to remain miserable is by comparing yourself to others. Sam is better at running than I am. Theresa speaks fluently when presenting compared to me. Samantha has a slim bikini body, way better than mine. It is obvious how comparing ourselves affects how we feel about ourselves.

I made it a rule to only compete with myself. In other words, I try to be better than who I was yesterday. This is way better than competing with someone else since you do not know the factors and inputs that led to what you covet in the other person. Even at that, we might falsely have this idea that their life is better while they paid through their nose to accomplish what we so desire.

Stop the Inner Critic

We all have that inner voice, and to improve our self-esteem, we need to be mindful of what our inner voice is telling us. That inner critic can be a motivation to pursue your goal, and it can also work against your self-esteem.

It is that inner critic that waters your mind with destructive thoughts. We all have them, common examples are:

- You cannot even do your job the right way, someone will notice and fire you soon.

- You do not have what it takes to be a good mother, our kids will turn out unruly.

- You are a bad wife, your husband will notice this and throw you out.

One thing I need you to know and accept is that these are mere suggestions without facts. There are helpful ways to challenge and minimize such damaging thoughts and replace it with something encouraging. You could literally tell yourself to stop when the thought springs up. It does not stop here because you might not really be able to silence your thoughts. However, what we recommend is replacing such thoughts with healthy ones.

Reflect on the Things You are Grateful for

This is one of the healthiest ways to improve your self-esteem. It is simple and can make a huge difference if you make it a habit. All you need do is set some time apart and reflect on the things you are grateful for. These are the simple things of life, not necessarily huge and things.

For instance, here is a list of three things I am grateful for:

- The ability to solve people's problem via writing.

- Being able to offer words of encouragement and motivation to others.

- For my understanding and supportive wife.

As you can see, they do not have to be significant things. You could be grateful for the ability to take a hike to improve your fitness rather than being lazy. It could be for the blessing of your cute and obedient children and how their smiles always lighten up your day. Not only does this habit build up your self-esteem, but it can also fill you with positive vibes and make you a happy person.

Invest Your Time with Supportive and Less Destructive People

Your quest to improve your self-esteem is not complete without being careful of the kind of company you keep. You might have done everything advised above, such as being kind to yourself, silencing the critic in you, and ending the comparison cycle. However, if you are constantly with people who make you question your choice, your effort will not yield any fruit.

With the above in mind, be sure to do away with people that do not support your quest to improve your self-esteem. In other words, the people you spend time with should have a realistic standard and encourage you to be kinder to yourself. It is not always about physical interactions. You have to be careful of what you absorb from the media as well. Internet and social media could be the perfect ground for unhealthy comparison. It is best you limit your consumption.

Identify and Develop Your Skills

One of the cheapest ways to build self-esteem is identifying what you are good at and continuing to develop it. In other words, identify your skills, abilities, and areas of your life that are very important and developing it. For instance, if you are a good basketball player, developing yourself such that you can feature in the college basketball team will build your confidence level, thereby building your self-esteem.

If you love helping people, sign up for volunteer causes, seek to help the aged and less privileged. The satisfaction that you will derive from this can help boost your self-esteem. The idea is to discover what you are good at and find opportunities to develop it.

Feel Comfortable Accepting Compliments

We tend to be so hard on ourselves such that we feel we are not worthy to accept compliments. However, receiving compliments can help develop self-esteem as it makes you feel good about yourself and your accomplishments. This, in turn, builds your confidence, which translates to improving social skills.

Even if the compliment makes you uncomfortable, prepare your mind, and have a ready-made response when you get such compliments. With time, the urge to deny and belittle the complements will fade, which is a good indication that your self-esteem is growing.

Overcoming Shyness

Many people struggle with shyness, even those who we wouldn't consider shy by any means. Even though it might feel like you are the only one, it is a pretty common issue. In the quest to improve your social skills, getting rid of shyness is one of the steps you need to take. However, getting rid of shyness does not happen overnight. You have taken the first step in picking up this manual.

I do not intend on boring you with the run-through of what shyness is or how it can affect you. I am pretty sure you are already aware of this which is why you picked up this manual. I once struggled with shyness and know how agonizing it can be. Then, my default move, which I am certain many people can relate to, wass to avoid all forms of social interaction. Many people interpret this wrongly yet, the victim suffers more as he has to deal with the uncomfortable and timid feeling that comes with shyness.

Without a doubt, shyness gets in the way of your interaction with other people. It affects your relationship and could end up leaving you dissatisfied with life. This is why this section of the book will shed light on practical ways to get rid of shyness. Note that it is a process which involves time, patience, and willingness.

How can you get rid of shyness?

Take Deep Breaths

Deep breathing, even though it sounds simple, can work wonders in helping you relax. All you need is a deep, full-bodied breath. Suck the air in and hold it for four seconds. Do this as many times as possible before facing the situation (interviews, presentations, dates, etc.) that makes you uncomfortable.

Taking a deep breath has a way of forcing the body to relax, even in the face of situations that seem life-threatening. Be sure not to engage in deep breathing where it seems obvious and can be misconstrued as a sigh, which could then send the wrong message. You can do this quietly when the other party is talking. It must not be conspicuous.

Always Assume a Good Posture

In communication and every form of interaction you have, the way you carry yourself is as important as what you say. In other words, be mindful of the message you are unconsciously passing with your body. Even though you are fighting shyness and timidity, you can assume a power pose that will make you come off as confident.

The simple things you can do about this is by ensuring you are mindful of the way you dress. Make sure you are always neat and presentable. Make sure you hold your head up always and keep your shoulders high.

Make Eye Contact

As a shy person, we acknowledge that eye contact can be unnerving. However, the world will not come crashing down at you if you make eye contact. Eye contact goes a long way in building confidence and establishing a connection.

You can start by looking at yourself in the mirror and practice talking to yourself while maintaining eye contact. With time, practice with your siblings or spouse and when you feel you are ready, launch yourself out there.

Learn to Smile

I was once a shy person, and people have mislabeled me as cold and unfriendly. I will not blame them. Someone told me I move about with a straight face, always minding my business. This is typical of shy people. However, smiling is an easy way to improve your life and make yourself approachable.

It costs you nothing and can be pretty helpful in acknowledging the other person. It passes you off as a friendly, welcoming, and approachable individual and can help set the mood for a great conversation. Even if this feels awkward or strange, practice before putting yourself out there.

With time, this will be second nature, and you will discover that you are making people's day better with your smile.

Be Kind to Yourself

You will not overcome shyness overnight. However, the most important thing is that you are making an effort to overcome it. Do not be alarmed of how long it takes as long as you are making progress. Besides the fact that you are working towards your goal, you are sensitive enough to know how you are doing. No matter how slow you feel or how your progress is, resist the temptation to beat yourself up as it could end up delaying your effort.

Deliberately Put Yourself Forward

As I reiterated in the opening paragraph, shyness cannot be wished away. You have to be deliberate in your effort to overcome shyness. One of the ways you can help yourself is by deliberately putting yourself in situations that make you uncomfortable. I know this is asking for too much, but it will help you.

Raise your hand and ask a question at the next Sunday school gathering. Volunteer to deliver the next seminar at work, invite a few friends for a dinner party. The idea is to do something, anything that will get you out of your comfort zone. The idea is to challenge your shyness and force it out. You might mess up at times , but that is okay. However, do not use that as an excuse to recoil back to your shell. Rather, take baby steps and face the challenges step by step. With time, you will discover a method that feels natural for you.

Chapter 2

Non-Verbal Communication

The Importance of Body Language

B ody language is a better judge of what a person is trying to pass along without verbal communication. There is a famous saying that states that actions speak louder than words, and it is true. It is crucial to pay attention to the body language, as it is the only way one can read between the lines. At times, one can communicate without saying one word. For instance, one can shrug their shoulders and inform you that they do not agree or do not understand what is going on.

In the process of communication, it has been shown that nonverbal communication contributes about 65-93% of the communication process. I mean that how someone says something means more than what they say. In as much as body language is an integral part of communication, one still has to prepare. You might want to communicate one thing and end up delivering the opposite because of fear or anxiety. It also means that one has to be very attentive to body language. Receivers of information are very sensitive to nonverbal cues one is sending.

a. *Overall Impression*

Body language is essential because it gives the overall impression. For instance, one might think that body language is only an additional point when looking for a job. However, it is everything, as it determines how interviewers view someone. It is crucial, and gives provides an impression of someone. Poor body language can create an environment where one is viewed in a certain way, and it traps them in that circle.

First impressions are usually striking and noticeable. It means that how other employees and employers see a person on the first day is the way he is viewed throughout his tenure at the workplace. Thus, one has to pay attention to their body language. One needs to pay attention to the way people around use body language in passing a message. In social settings and other aspects of life, it will help one know when to make their next move. In a world where social networks are the currency, it can help one navigate the social space seamlessly.

Body language is controlled by the brain, which means that one might pretend as they communicate verbally. But the subconscious will always betray them. For instance, one can pretend to listen to a statement, but be fidgety. It demonstrates a lack of interest, anxiety, or poor concentration. It is not easy to have proper body language, especially in stressful situations.

b. *Controls brain perception of a person*

Another famous quote when it comes to body language is that practice makes perfect. This is entirely true when people with adept social skills are examined. It is also right in the workplace, with people who are well-liked or receive promotions. Body language is not an innate ability- it is leaned, which means that it can be sharpened over time. This means that one has to practice their body language in daily social interactions to improve it.

Body language affects how people view themselves, according to Amy Cudder. If someone practices to be authoritative, then the brain receives signals that model it to create the impression that one is more authoritative. Thus, one ends up being more confident. Therefore, to develop such skills, one should learn how to be authoritative, as it helps the brain produce a perception about themselves. Positive nonverbal communication not only helps one appear more authoritative, but it also helps them seem to have more control of the situation.

The same way our minds control our bodies; it is the same way our bodies regulate our bodies. Thus, body language is essential because it can be used as a tool to control your mind. If you fear to speak before other people, one practices speaking to audiences for some while. This gets them used to it eventually. It is only until then that they will get the confidence to speak in front of people.

Body language behaves the same way when one wants to project a particular message nonverbally. They have to bite the bullet and speak in front of people until they have mastered the body language. Body language plays a crucial role in relationships, career, and everyday life Thus, paying attention to body language is bound to bring good results in every aspect of life.

22

c. *Enables one to read between the lines*

The ability to pick on negative body language can help one pick on nonverbal cues that communicate bad feelings. In a social setting, this is very important, because it enables one to know when to answer, and how to respond in a conversation. This is especially true when communicating with a senior. For instance, one has to deal with a customer who is not very welcoming. Body language will help one navigate the conversation according to what is being communicated non verbally.

It will also help one to know when to engage, and when to leave issues alone. It is a crucial negotiation skill that is often looked over, as it helps one understand the best times to communicate an item they desire.

d. *Communicate sensitive information in public spaces*

In social situations, body language can be used to pass secrets and ensure that the secrets are not received by anyone else in the same social setting. Language is risky to use, especially if one wants some information to remain private. In the era of recording devices and Google translate, using a different language is not enough to keep information private. Therefore coded body language has to be used effectively to pass on information to the necessary people.

For instance, a group of people in a competition can agree that touching the nose can mean that they take a particular move. Thus, having such inside information can help then have a competitive advantage over their peers. It can also help in the passing of sensitive information. A gesture from one party can help a group understand the piece of knowledge.

In highly sensitive matters such as combat, body language can be used to mislead the enemy, and keep troops safe. Thus, body language can be used to communicate specific sets of information that a group does not want to be interpreted with another group.

Identifying People's Non-Verbal Cues and Being Aware of Your Own

Non-verbal cues do not have a direct verbal translation. And there is no single gesture that is self-sufficient to communicate what a person feels when they manifest them entirely. Hence, it is important to pay attention to as many cues possible than just one. On the surface of it, the objective of reading bodily cues is to be able to tell whether one is comfortable in their current situation. Blending cues with contexts that the subject person is in helps in reading their thoughts, hence putting more meaning into the deciphered messages.

The better you understand how people encode their feelings and thoughts into cues and how to decode them, the more aware you become at encrypting yours. You begin communicating your specific bodily messages more precisely. It takes quite some effort learning them and practicing them out till you are there. There are many physical cues with as many meanings too, and here we will bring you only some of them. Individualities are different, and sometimes, under similar circumstances, each will display different gestures, or for the very ones, send a different message altogether. By observing the suggested patterns for gestures, you are bound to get it right eventually.

Depending on the nature of the meeting, you can deduce whether one is dressed for success, epitomizes ambition, or are casual. You can also judge if they are comfortable or are being seductive or are portraying spiritual values. There is a message in their choice appearance, and beyond what they might want to say by it, it tells further whether they are in sync with the purpose of the meeting.

Pay attention to their posture too. Walking with head held high tells of confidence while a certain kind of slow walk can depict them as being indecisive or cowardly, probably due to low self-esteem. The chest pushed forward with expanded hands is a show of one who is full of themselves, a big-ego.

Expansive poses show the power and a sense of achievement. People hold themselves according to how they are feeling. Feeling of power and being in control is depicted in a leaned back relaxed posture. Maintaining an erect position, walking purposefully with palms down in an open, expansive body is an authoritative posture signaling your leadership ambition or capability.

We tend to close in and lean toward the people we like but keep a distance or lean away from those we do not prefer. This can, however, be affected by cultures. By crossing our arms or legs, we show that we are defensive, angry, or protective of ourselves. When it is the legs that are crossed, we tend to point the big toe of the foot on top toward the person with whom we are at ease.

Crossed legs also mean that someone is being resistant, unreceptive, and can be a bad sign in negotiation. It depicts their mental, emotional, and physical closure, and unwillingness to budge in bargaining. Lip biting and cuticle picking are soothing when individuals find themselves under pressure or in awkward situations.

Emotions naturally etch on the face. A deep frown, for instance, indicates that one is worrying or over-thinking.

A person facing away from you during conversation means they are bored, disinterested, or are being deceitful. When they look down, they could be nervous or submissive. Good eye contact and dilated pupil is a sign of interest in the conversation and in the person that you are interacting with. A faster blinking is characteristic when one is thinking, stressed, or lying. We also glance at people in whom we are interested. A lie has just been told when the person looks upward then right. If they look upward then left, the statement they just made may have some truth.

Is one holding unusually more prolonged eye contact with you? Probably, they do not want to look shifty-eyed. In attempts to avoid fidgeting, they may also still themselves for too long when standing or seated or not blink. These gestures can be consciously manipulated to hide their lying intentions.

Genuine smiles engage the whole face. Faked smiles imply shallow contradictory pleasure or approval while half-smiles are sarcastic or show uncertainty. A grimace before a smile is a sign of hidden dissatisfaction. Facial displays of emotion if they are not bilateral, are faked. Genuine smiles, for instance, are symmetrical.

When one nods slowly, it means they are interested and want to listen more to your talk. Fast nodding says one has heard enough and wants you to finish or give them a chance to respond. One tilts their head sideways in concentration to the conversation but tilts it backward in suspicion or uncertainty. We also tend to face people we are interested in, or we have an affinity with. Exaggerated nodding implies anxiety about approval. When one is not sure what you are thinking about them or are unsure whether they will execute your command, they nod excessively.

People shrug their shoulders when they have no clue what is going on. This gesture comprises exposed arms to show openness, hunched shoulders for neck protection in case there is a possible threat, and raised brows of submission. Raised eyebrows alone show discomfort. Worry, surprise, or fear can trigger this gesture. So a compliment, for instance, with raised eyebrows can be insincere.

When one laughs with you and is interested in your humor during a conversation, it is likely to be that they find your personality to be amazing. Mirrored body language means the conversation is progressing well and signals a feeling of connection between the two of you.

Does one seem sad, and their inner corners of the eyebrows do not move up and in? Then they are not as miserable as they seem. Reluctance to express specific thoughts and emotions can be shown by sucked in lips. One 'wipes away' a problem or concern by wiping their face down. Holding the chin in the fist says one is objected to what has just been said.

Establishing Trust

Non-verbal cues can enable you to establish the level of trust between yourself and the person you are communicating with. By simply studying elements of people's body language, you will be able to know whether or not you can trust them. This is because there are elements of the non-verbal communication that tell you when a person is lying. Others hint to a person speaking the truth. For instance, a person who can maintain eye-contact for a considerable period is likely to be telling the truth as compared to someone who finds it difficult to maintain the same. This, therefore, implies that when you are interacting with someone, you should always focus on their eyes. Try to establish if they are looking directly at you or they seem to be looking away.

Similarly, on your part, it is important to ensure that you are able to maintain eye-contact while communicating with others. If you are able to maintain good eye contact throughout the conversation, you will come across as somebody who is confident and trustworthy.

Non-verbal Cues and Rapport

Good rapport can enable you to establish effective relationships with other people, both within your social and professional circles. Good rapport refers to positivity on your part that can easily rub off on other people. When you have a good rapport with someone else, they will want to spend more time with you, share their experiences with you, and trust you with their resources such as money.

While interacting with someone else, it is essential to look out for non-verbal cues that can let you know whether or not you have a good rapport with them. One of the most notable elements of non-verbal cues with respect to the rapport that you can look out in other people is the tendency to lean forward when talking to you. If someone prefers to lean forward every time they are interacting with you, it indicates that they like you. You can quickly establish a good rapport with them.

The tendency by other people to point their arms towards you can also let you know that you have a good rapport with them. You could be in the presence of other people, and one person seems to be constantly pointing towards you with their head or hands. They are letting others know that they have a high opinion of you. On the other hand, if someone looks away from you and does not point at you, then you might experience a difficult time establishing a good rapport with them.

On your part, you should also identify aspects of non-verbal cues that can enhance rapport between you and the people around you. First and foremost, you should always point or look at someone when talking to them. The reason is that; the other person will appreciate the fact that you recognize their presence and their role in the whole affair.

Always Keep Your Chin Up

The position of your chin while walking or interacting with other people is an essential pointer to the kind of image that you are trying to portray. When you walk around with your chin facing downwards, people may perceive it as a sign of timidity or cowardice. On the other hand, if you walk around with your chin upwards, other people will see you as a confident person who can be dependent on. It is therefore vital to ensure that you always maintain your chin up whenever talking or interacting with other people to send the right message.

Avoid Fidgeting

Fidgeting is a form of nervous motion that will make you seem uncomfortable and nervous. To this end, you should remember not to fidget while interacting with other people. Instead, you should maintain a confident demeanor with minimum unnecessary movements. Furthermore, fidgeting can also interfere with the concentration of the person you are talking to. When you keep on fidgeting while interacting with others, they are more likely to spend more time focusing on your involuntary movements as opposed to full concentrating on what you are saying.

Do not put your Hands in Your Pocket

Placing your hands in your pockets is considered an unnatural pose while interacting with someone. Most often than not, putting your hands in your pocket could tell the other person that you lack the much-needed self-confidence or that you are anxious. On the other hand, keeping your hands out of your pockets is considered a reassuring pose that can tell the other person that you know what you are talking about.

Firm Handshake

When it comes to handshakes, they must always be firm. A firm handshake is one of the most blatant displays of confidence. When you can hold the hand of the person you are greeting firmly, you will send across a message that you are confident about yourself. It compels others to take you seriously. A weak handshake can make you come across as someone with low self-confidence. A weak handshake might also encourage opportunistic people to try and take advantage of you. To this end, you should always ensure that your handshake is firm even when you feel intimidated by the person you are meeting. It will conceal your discomfort and fear, thus enhancing your self-confidence in the process.

Lean Forward

Leaning forward tells the person you are talking to that you are interested in their point of view. When you are discussing something with someone else, you should lean forward to make them know that you are listening and willing to know more. It is an essential aspect of non-verbal cues if you are not necessarily interested in what the other person is saying. For instance, you might be interacting with your child, who is not saying anything meaningful. When you lean forward, the child will know that you are interested in them.

Finally, being aware of the non-verbal cues of others is vital in enabling you to understand them better. Non-verbal cues can give you information that the other person is not willing to share, and as they say, information is power. When you have such information at your fingertips, you can make better and informed decisions. Similarly, you should also be aware of your non-verbal cues. You should never overlook elements of your non-verbal cues since you are continually sending out messages even when you do not know. Being aware of your non-verbal cues will enable you to send out the right message that will work to your advantage.

Chapter 3

Communication

Learn How to Make a Proper Introduction

I ntroducing yourself to someone you have never met is often the hardest part of being in a conversation with strangers. Rarely will you hear someone say, "Oh how I love the excitement of walking up to strangers and introducing myself." Most of us are very apprehensive about introducing ourselves to strangers.

Be Bold and Take the Initiative

Have you ever noticed how when we walk into new places where we know no one, we stand to the side and start assessing — with prejudice — the strangers to determine who seems friendly and approachable? This is why, for instance, when you attend a networking event, you will see tons of people pressed against the wall with phone in hand and heads bowed. The same applies to a public area such as the train. You will notice many seated at the corner or edges of their seats with their heads down or focused on other things.

Instead of following suit, boldly walk into any room or area full of strangers with confidence while assessing who looks interesting. Now use the outward focus strategy we discussed in step 1 to look for people you have a commonality with.

Another great trick is to look for cues that signal an interesting conversation ahead. For instance, if you are attending a networking event where everyone looks crisp and clean dressed in a suit and tie, and you notice someone in a beach shirt and flip-flops, this could be the signal for a great conversation because this person must have an interesting reason for going against the grain.

Once you find such a person, because many people are cagey about introducing themselves, center yourself and gather the courage to say a hello. This brings us to the next topic ...

Shake Hands or Say Hello

The easiest way to introduce yourself is to offer your hand for a greeting or say hello. Extending your hand for a greeting is better because it makes you seem approachable, warm, friendly, and confident. This may seem like an awkward step, but we have been trained subconsciously to reciprocate a handshake when another person extends his/her hand. This has become an accepted line of social interaction so don't fear. However, if your hands are perspiring, something relatively common in those afraid of conversing with strangers, you can say hello and continue the conversation from there.

As you shake hands, resist the temptation to squeeze the hand too tightly In no one's mind is a crushing handshake enjoyable. In the same breath do not offer a limp handshake, what we call a wet fish handshake because such a handshake speaks of low confidence. Aim to strike a balance between the two.

Maintain Eye Contact

This is the most important part of approaching a stranger. Walk into a room, scan and notice a stranger you would like to engage in conversation. As you walk towards that person to introduce yourself with a handshake, hello, and some pleasantries, maintain eye contact especially if the person is looking at you as you approach. This will portray confidence, which will draw the interest of the other person.

Moreover, as you shake the person's hand, maintain eye contact. This shows you are present and ready for an interesting interaction. Other than humanizing yourself, good eye contact allows you to read body language cues that you can then use to create rapport

Attentively Listen

Nervousness causes many to monopolize a conversation, ramble or even over talk. For example, if you are anxious and nervous, after shaking someone's hand and saying something like "Hi, I'm X or Y," you may blubber on without giving the person a chance to introduce him or herself to you. This does not bode well in fostering a good conversation. Feeling heard is a core human need. If you deny the other person a chance to discuss the things he or she cares about, the conversation you are trying to start will be over before you get past the pleasantries.

After saying hi and introducing yourself by name, give the other person a chance to reciprocate and once the person tells you his or her name, remember it and use it during the conversation.

Using these four strategies, you can introduce yourself to anyone.

Tips to have a conversation

Make small talk.

Sociologists have a rule that indicates that the best way to create a fluid conversation is to keep one important rule in mind: 30% talking and 70% listening. This is a general rule, and obviously, it will change from situation to situation, so keep that in mind. But in general terms, this will make you an interesting person to talk to, because you will pay attention and ask correct and specific questions. This, in due time, will make you a desirable person to talk to.

At the end of a conversation, don't forget to introduce yourself

This is only applicable if it is a first-time conversation, but it is a great way to ensure that the other person knows and remembers your name. Try to say something like "By the way, I'm…" More often than not, the other person will do the same. Always remember names, because that is a great way to make impressions on people. You will be more inclined to talk to someone who remembered your name or anything else that you told them. Also, if you remember their name, you will not only look smart and intelligent, but they will see that you were paying attention.

Ask them out for coffee

We talked about this tip before, but it is important to expand on this. A social gathering gives you a better opportunity to truly know another person, in a way that perhaps might not be possible in another context. Invite them to get some coffee or to go to the theater. To organize and plan with them, you can give them your phone number or email address.

This gives them the possibility to contact you at any time. Don't worry if they don't give you their information in return, because that's fine. There will be time for that in the future, once you get to know each other. One handy way to extend your invitation is to say something along the lines of "I gotta go, but what about we go out some time, maybe to get coffee or for lunch? Here's my phone number if you ever want to call me." Perhaps they don't have enough time to make new friends. I mentioned this before - don't take it personally. Offer your contact information to people who have the potential to be a good friend, and in time, somebody will get back to you.

These steps are clear, direct, and simple. But like every step that we talked about in this book, while this might help, it doesn't replace professional help. If you feel like you can't implement these steps, and no matter what you do, you can't make new friends, then the best solution is to seek professional help. Going to a shrink isn't a big deal, and there is absolutely no shame in it. Do what you can to get better, and the first step to do it is to deal with it.

Dull Conversations

Congratulations, the guy you talked to called to see if that invitation for coffee was still on. You have a new friend! So you both decide on a date, place, and activity. The appointment comes, you sit down to talk and get to know each other, and then you notice that the conversation dies as soon as one of you stops talking. No matter how hard you both try, ultimately, the conversation dies. Even if you go back to your main passion (the one you talked about the first time), the dullness and repetitiveness bore you both. After a while, one of you decides to call it a night and go home. You go home confused. What happened? Everything seemed to be going great the first time, what happened the second time?

Dull conversations are the main obstacle that you will face when you try to form a new relationship with anybody. It is something that you have to actively fight in every conversation, and if it is left unchecked, it will poison the bond that you have with that particular person. But the way to confront this is quite easy, and if you practice every day, you will become an expert at handling this.

In my experience, the best way to engage and create a fun environment for conversations is to find out what turns people on. No, I do not mean it that way, I'm talking about being turned on emotionally. This is the first step that you have to take, and at the same time the hardest, because you will be blind in this. The idea behind this step of the conversation is to find out what stimulates the other person on an emotional level, and as the name suggests, it might get emotional. Never talk about heavy subjects, at least in the first few times. If the other person needs to talk about a certain heavy subject, the subject will come up naturally. You can use this heavy subject list as a guide to see what is best to avoid:

- Abortion and health-related topics

- Religion (this is quite an important one, particularly because many people see religion as a way of life, so, unless you both share the same religion, try to avoid this one at all cost)

- Politics

- In some cases: Sports

While the rest might be quite obvious, you might be thinking that sports shouldn't be on that list, but the truth is that many people take sports way too seriously and will defend their colours or team with a passion. Unless you are knowledgeable on the subject, it's best to stay away from this topic.

Other subjects might be off the table depending on the case (for example, if you see that your interlocutor has a disability, don't bring that up unless the subject comes up naturally), but in general terms, the list should help you stay clear of any problems. With that being said, if your values are rooted in those subjects (you might have a firm opinion on abortion or current politics), always be aware that while people might have an opinion on it, it does not mean that they necessarily want to share it.

We talked about finding out what the other person loves. One quick way to break the social rule or norm that might rule over the conversation (like small talk) is to stop using social scripts or if possible, avoid asking questions that society makes us feel like we need to ask. To do this, go out of your way to learn about that person's life:

- "What has been the best part of your year?"
- "What do you as a hobby?"
- "Leaving work aside, what is your main objective during the day?"

According to several researchers on the topic, what guides our relationships and our interaction with the rest of the world is to feel important, to feel cherished, and to find other interesting people. This is normal, and this does not mean that we are all selfish (although if you need this a bit too much, you may end up having an egocentric personality, so be careful). The psychology behind this is quite straightforward: if you can make someone feel unique and special by listening and paying attention to their opinions, feelings or ideas, you will in turn become attractive to them.

When you talk to someone and want to show them your appreciation, you can try to ask them questions to find out what they believe to be significant. When they give you an answer, you can push their ideas a little further. This is tricky: Let's say that you ask them about what they love the most in the world. Their answer is "Carpentry". In this particular case, you could ask them why and how that thing or action (Carpentry) is important for them. But this does not mean that you can push them around. Don't go hard on them. Remember, you are trying to be interesting, so avoid being aggressive.

If you are talking to someone at a party, try to commit to them entirely. Don't stay on your phone or talk to anyone other than the person you are talking to at that moment. If you dedicate your entire attention to that specific person, they will feel important and worthy of attention and do their best to earn it. Smile if it is a good story, laugh if it is funny, or show sadness if it is a sad story. Don't take a trip to the bathroom so you can check emails or upload a picture to the internet. People will eventually realize this and may stop talking to you. After all, their time is important so why would they bother with someone who doesn't value it?

Your posture is also a window into your interest in the other person. People unconsciously pick up body signs that show us that people pay attention to them, or that they are ignoring them. Other than avoiding to check your phone, the following are several tips that you might not know about:

The direction of your toes. Yes, it sounds quite silly, but as I said, this is one of those signs that we pick up without even knowing. If you keep your toes pointed to the person speaking, their brains will pick up your feet direction and use that sign to gauge interest. If you are listening to someone talk about their experiences as a father, you can make them feel valued and worthy of your attention by keeping your torso and toes pointed at them while they speak. It's a non-verbal way to express interest and say "go on, I'm listening".

The triple nod is a way of expressing interest. It might sound weird at first, but studies have proved that people tend to speak two to four times longer if you give them a triple nod. This works as a subconscious cue to keep going and expand their story. When someone finishes talking, and you feel that there might be more in it, look at them in their eyes and nod three times. More times than not, they will continue their story, and if they don't, you can always ask another question related to what they have been talking about.

If you see that the conversation is dying, ask open-ended questions. This will help to keep the conversation alive. For example, let's say that your interlocutor is talking about old Roman History, and you see that the discussion is reaching a phase where both of you don't know what to say.

In that case, ask something that might take a while to fully answer. In the example that we were talking about, ask about the differences between Romans and Greeks, and how each civilization adapted to the other. Keep in mind that I'm just giving random examples based on conversations that I had in the past, and you can always ask whatever you want. This will help to avoid "yes" and "no" answers, allow your interlocutor to express himself, and share more information that you can use to continue the conversation.

Perhaps this is the perfect time to mention it, but conversations shouldn't be like a police interrogation. While a bit of questioning is fine, it can't be at the expense of your interlocutor's peace. I suggested furthering the conversation a bit more, but never push it to the point that you make the other person feel uncomfortable. If they don't want to answer a question, or they wish to go somewhere else to talk or do something else, let them be. They don't owe you an answer, and if they don't want to speak, they are under no obligation to do so. During my times reading and watching people interact, I've seen several awkward people forcing their views and their opinions over the rest because they wrongly believed that the primary goal of any conversation is to win the argument. This is an absolute mistake and one you should avoid at all costs.

Other things that you can use to start and keep a conversation alive is to talk about something special that they are wearing or something particular about the environment you are both in. In the story that I told you before, my friend's wife asked her about the t-shirt. This is a perfect way to start a conversation because if they are wearing a unique piece of clothing, they will be more inclined to talk about it. Or if they have another unique piece of clothing, like special earrings, for example, it can spark a conversation about where they got them and if they got them during a trip overseas. However, if they don't have anything in particular, you can always comment on your environment, and use it as a cue to talk about anything that comes to your mind. Say that at the party that you are both in, there are distinctive candles lighting up the place. In that case, you can comment that they remind you of the candles that your grandmother used to use (or whatever it tells you; of course, you do not have to follow precisely what I write here!). This, in turn, will create a snowball effect in the conversation and keep the ball rolling.

Keep practicing these steps, and with enough practice, you will see that in every conversation that you have, you will end up going far more in-depth than you expected.

But let's go down the negative road: No matter what you try, the conversation dies. You did everything you could, and you have to understand that you are under no obligation to like every single person you meet in your life. You may create a lasting relationship with some of them, and the rest will come and go from your life. That is okay, and the best solution in these cases is to retreat and move over to another person who you might feel more connected to or have more things in common with.

Keep the Conversation Going Past the Pleasantries

One of the most terrifying things about being in a conversation, especially with strangers, is the awkward silence many of us experience after engaging in a fair amount of small talk.

The awkward silence is something that causes many not to take the plunge into conversation. Now that you have overcome the fear of talking to strangers, introduced yourself in the nicest way possible, and through conversation starters engaged in a fair amount of small talk, the next challenge is the challenge of never running out of things to say. How do we continue the conversation while keeping it interesting and flowing?

To overcome this problem, the first thing you need to understand is why the awkward silence happens, especially when you are conversing with strangers. The awkward silence is internal because when you think you have run out of things to say that is exactly what is happening. You have activated a filter that sifts through what you think is good enough to say to a stranger thus limiting your choices.

This filter is almost nonexistent when you are conversing with people you know well. You can converse for hours about different unrelated topics without stressing over what to say next. Your "good enough for conversation" threshold is very low when speaking to a friend or acquaintance. If you feel like bringing up an interesting topic that pops into your mind, you just do.

Therein lies the answer to keeping a conversation going past the pleasantries. You must lose your inhibitions and not filter things out of your conversation. As long as a topic or thought is good enough to vocalize, do so. You need to learn how to adapt to conversations on the go, which you can do by removing this filter.

In addition to keeping the conversation going past the small talk and pleasantries, you need to be emotionally vulnerable. This does not mean you need to reveal your deepest darkest secret. All it means is that you have to lead first by opening up first. Be the first one to move the conversation past the pleasantries by sharing something personal. Here is why this is important.

You will pick up a few things about the other person when you are attentive. Even so, you cannot outright ask a stranger to tell you his or her darkest secrets. After all, you would not expect someone you just met to ask the same of you. You are likely to be more trusted when you are vulnerable and share

something about yourself to the other person first. When people feel trusted, they reciprocate in kind. Because you have opened yourself up to them, they will open themselves up to you, which will take the conversation deeper.

Another way to take conversations past the pleasantries is to concentrate on the types of topics you bring up as you engage in small talk. In most cases, most of us have 10 or so questions we ask and when the stranger we are talking to answers most of these, an awkward silence ensues.

Here, you need to concentrate on using conversation prompts that call for more than one word answers. For instance, questions such as "how is work", "how are the kids" or "how have you been" will do very little to take the conversation past the surface. This is why you need to bring up weighty topics for discussion. Keep the conversation deep and interesting but avoid certain subject matters such as death or war. Our goal is to keep these conversations fun. Talking about death or war is certainly not fun.

Important and serious topics will foster a more interesting and engaging conversation. You will learn a lot about the other person by sharing impactful stories related to the topic in discussion. You will also have managed to take the conversation past the pleasantries.

Learn How to Turn Strangers Into Friends

The greatest of things come to those who are willing to risk rejection and failure. The fear of rejection is the very thing that has been keeping you from creating lasting friendships and relationships with strangers. Now that you have implemented steps 1 through 5, you have overcome this fear. Congratulations! You are now ready for the challenge of turning one off chance conversation with a stranger into a lasting friendship. Here is how to do that:

Build on the Commonalities

At this point, we shall assume that the stranger you want to turn into a friend is someone you have engaged in small talk, and after deepening the conversation, matching and mirroring, have decided that this person is someone worth making a friend.

To keep this conversation going and the friendship flourishing, you can build on commonalities. For instance, if both you and the stranger/acquaintance like hiking, and you and several other friends have planned a hike in the coming weeks or month, you can casually invite this person and then continue deepening the conversation on this point of mutual interest. Because the person likes hiking, he or she is more likely to say yes, and this will offer you a chance to meet the person for a second time. This future interaction will cement the acquaintance and turn it into a budding friendship.

Don't Forget the Contact Information

After having a great first conversation with someone you just met, before you go your separate ways, read the situation. If you feel that the person had a great time conversing with you (especially if, in the earlier example, the person agrees to come for the planned hike), take the initiative and ask for contact information.

Having contact information of your "new friend" is going to make communication easier for when you plan to meet up again. When it comes to asking for contact information, just be direct. Say something like, "I had so much fun chatting with you. Before you go, let's exchange numbers so we can get together and chat more about that hike."

Be Friendly

In more than one occasion, we have indicated that acquaintances feel more attracted to us, and thus more open to friendships, if we are open and vulnerable at a personal level. This is what we mean by being friendly. Once you navigate through steps 1-5 of connecting with a stranger, that person is no longer a stranger, he or she is an acquaintance, which is a step away from friendship. Treat such a person as you would treat a friend, which means you should embark on creating a level of honest communication and familiarity while discussing and acting on mutual interests.

Learn How to Become the Center of Attention

Now that you are coming to the end of this 7 step guide, you need to learn one more skill: how to become the center of attention. If you have noticed, the first 6 steps of this guide have a central theme: outward concentration on the person at the other end of the conversation.

Naturally, there are instances where you will want to hog attention when in a social situation. For instance, if we go with our hiking example from step 6, when you, your new friend and other friends do finally go for that hike, you may want to be the center of attention so you can keep the conversation going and keep your new friend from feeling left out. Here are several ways to do that:

Assume a Central Position

If you are attending a social gathering, one effective way to attract attention is to stand or sit at a prominent position where attention is centrally focused. Perhaps stand in the center of the room and then ask your friends to join you there or seat yourself in the middle of the table. This will make you appear friendly and approachable, which means strangers will feel drawn to you.

Move Periodically

Continuing with the social gathering example, even after assuming a central location, do not cement yourself there, which is what many of us tend to do. Instead, move positions at intervals of 15-30 minutes. This ensures you interact with as many people as possible, which also means you will end up attracting a lot of good attention.

Be the Conversation Starter

We have talked about the importance of being the bold one. You have to realize that most people shy away from starting a conversation. Therefore, if you are the one starting them, you will be "the one" reaching out to those around you. You will automatically become the center of attention. Moreover, remember to follow the rules of starting a conversation: keep the conversation light, and when you stumble upon someone or a group of interesting people, deepen the conversation, and rope in more people into the conversation.

Master the Art of Conversation

Like art, conversation is a skill of nuance, elegance, and creative implementations. There's an art to everything we do and without style, flair and practice, most things become labor.

You've probably come across many individuals who've mastered the art of conversation. From afar, these individuals often possess the ability to talk to anyone with ease, some are born skillful and gifted with a gift to gap, while others like you and have to practice to become eloquent conversationalists.

The art of conversation is an acquired skill that you learn from walking up to strangers without acting dramatic or being a comedian. Although there are many ways to master the art of conversation, below are a few exemplary ways:

How to Master the Art of Conversation

Be Yourself and Relax Your Body

When walking up to a stranger, don't pretend to be something or someone you're not.

When you try to be someone you are not, your body language will betray you by mirroring this deceit, meaning you'll have failed to start a conversation way before you get a chance to utter a word.

It's difficult to act relaxed when you're not and you may end up saying or doing incomprehensible things completely unrelated to your current conversation. To calm your nerves and relax your body, practice a slow walking pace and take several deep breaths and smile warmly to appear more pleasant and approachable.

When you're relaxed, act normal and friendly, it will make it easier for other people to open up and introduce themselves. If you aren't received well, understand there is a reason behind it and move on. Perhaps the stranger is not a conversation mood and your timing is bad.

Balance Between Talking And Listening:

If you want to have good, and enjoyable conversation with strangers, strike a balance between listening and talking. A conversation can turn from nice and smooth to boring if one party does all the talking while the other party simply listens. This can make the listening partner slowly tune out thus killing off the conversation. There're many reasons that may trigger the lack of a balanced conversation; nervousness is the main cause. Nervousness freezes you and makes it difficult to find something to say.

When this happens, take one deep breath, one after another, wear a smile on your face, and focus on whatever you were saying. If it's the other person who freezes up, try to interrupt them. If your effort fails to achieve the desired results, politely excuse yourself, and move on. To strike up good conversations, both conversing partners should equally and comfortably express themselves; otherwise, the conversation will turn into monologue.

Show Interest And Curiosity

To start genuine conversations that will last awhile, show interest first. Showing interest will help encourage the other person to feel comfortable with you, be relaxed, and interact with you freely.

Portray attentiveness and be curious through maintaining eye contact throughout the conversation, and listening keenly. This way, even if you're shy, you'll be able to approach a stranger and make it easier to strike up a friendship.

Be Interesting And Variably Knowledgeable

Being interesting doesn't mean becoming an entertainer, comedian, or a brilliant narrator. No. To be interesting, all you need is to show interest in others, be well-informed and up to date with current trends, and avoid any talk that revolves around you and your experiences.

Be updated on local and world news, events, latest music, technology and new discoveries. Since we can't know everything that goes on in our surroundings, the little you know can keep up your conversation and make it interesting while you learn new things as well. When you feel unqualified to say something, listen and smile while you enjoy the comedy and humor rather than act ill, at ease, or as someone who doesn't fit in.

Practice To Perfect

Like any art and skill, it takes practice to be good at anything including the art of conversation. Don't expect to be an expert after you've had your first few trials. A lot of practice, adjustments and different social situations exposure is necessary and the more you approach and converse with different people, the more you'll build your conversation skills.

Silence Your Inner Critic

Unfortunately, you will have moments when your inner critic keeps on slipping in some comments meant to bring you down as you converse with a stranger. Your inner critic will probably slip in such thoughts as he doesn't like me, I am so boring, he is just pretending, he is trying to be nice to me, he or she cannot be so nice to me; he must be hiding something. Such thoughts can make you anxious and lose words when conversing with a stranger. As such, you need to silence them if you are to have a meaningful conversation where there is no clear awkwardness during the conversation. To silence your inner critic, take a deep breath and challenge your inner critic by asking for evidence for whatever it is that your inner critic is saying.

Practice your conversation skills with people you feel comfortable with and family before venturing out to other social events. Practicing on your circle of friends will give you positive feedback that will allow you to identify your weaknesses and work on them.

To become skilled in the art of conversation, practice: there is nothing like too much practice.

Chapter 1

Recognize Social Anxiety and Shyness

I t is normal to feel nervous in some situations. But when the degree of the feeling of anxiety escalates to higher grades till you stay fearful, self-conscious and feel embarrassed always thinking that you are being judged or rated by others, then you could be suffering from social anxiety, also called social phobia. Socially anxious people possess fear and anxiety that makes them avoid people and situations and this ends up disrupting their lives. Their routines of work, school, home, and other activities become affected and maladjusted significantly. Social anxiety mainly chronically keeps dragging one's mental health and impacts negatively on their ability to develop their confidence and interact with people. The socially anxious are quite shy.

Different people exhibit different levels of comfort in different situations depending on their traits of personality and life experiences. As such, not every display of shyness in everyone, especially children, denotes socially anxiety. There could be more to pay attention to in order to arrive at such a conclusion. Even among the maturing and the adults, there are outgoing personalities and the withdrawn kinds of people who are not necessarily shy or socially anxious. Social anxiety sets in from the early years of one's teenage years, but it can also start earlier in the younger children as well as among the adults.

The socially anxious are always conscious of situations in which they may feel judged by other people. They perceive themselves from the eyes of everybody else and think that they will be seen as inadequate, hence want to stay away. They really are fearful that whatever they would do, say or present to people would make them embarrassed or humiliated before the people. They always foresee how the congregation would respond in a manner suggesting that they did not do well, or they just did it wrong.

The socially anxious have intense fear getting to interact or talk with strangers. They do not know how to initiate a conversation or even sustain a conversation with people they do not know. Oftentimes, they even fail to greet and might not respond audibly to greeting. The anxious know they are anxious. They really fear that everyone else will notice their anxiety by their looks or behaviours. They are uncertain how to carry themselves in a way to show their confidence, and this causes them more anxiety. This, further, causes them embarrassment and they begin to sweat, blush, tremble and their voice becomes shaky.

The socially anxious just end up avoiding speaking to people and doing things, however small, because they fear to embarrass themselves at it. They doubt their capability to carry on a sound conversation, to understand what is spoken to them, to use appropriate terms e.g. technical or professional, and are uncertain how appropriately they can respond and keep the conversation sound and alive. This is the very knowledge that makes them think they could become the centre of attention for everyone. They do not want to be the main presenters at an event, or to have a lengthy session addressing a group of people, or to become a subject upon which the rest can observe and learn or discuss issues.

Required to facilitate or perform at an event, the socially phobic will have a lot of fear in anticipation for the dreaded activity or event. The phobic are more inclined toward the thoughts of not getting or comprehending instructions right and therefore fear that they will not do it right. That forms their basis for fear of events where they need to be lead persons. When the event is at hand and they are at the activity, they really endure the sense of being alive to the world present with them. They are intensely fearful and anxious doing it and are consciously trying to avoid making mistakes or attracting congregational participation in the course of action. Just, it is not natural for them to be subject persons at anything good or bad. And they might even wonder why they had to be chosen in the first place.

At the end of the session, the socially phobic believe they never gave their all. They constantly think that they excluded something important, they included some unimportant stuff, they did not say something perfectly, they overemphasized a trivial point or activity etc. Then they start ruminating on that for a long-time post-event. They will identify flaws in their interactions with people and their activity and their presentations and prove to themselves why they should not have taken up the step in the first place, or how they could have perceived and performed things better.

Socially phobic people are akin to overthinkers. They expect negative things to arise in the course of every good action. When things seem not to go as well planned or intended it is normal to them. When it all goes well, it is strange. Now negative anticipation is not just it to the phobic – overthinkers by now. Negative events are anticipated to yield the worst possible outcomes. A socially phobic will expect not to be agreeable to by their counterpart, and beyond that, they will perceive a possible conflict that could quickly ensue into a fight or exchange of abuses. This imagined experience will make them want to stay away from trouble by staying away from people, or just not expressing themselves at all.

Social anxiety in children may manifest in the form of crying, throwing tantrums, clinging closely and strictly to their caretakers and refusing to talk to everybody, including their very caretakers. They will hide their face away on the caretakers. A socially anxious child can even run away from home and end up in odd places – streets or in the bushes or plantations. They fear coming face to face with people and fear the consequence of not being able to speak up, which could be punishment, that they cannot mentally withstand.

Physically, socially phobic people blush a lot. They do not know how to acknowledge appreciation, and they do not as well know how to cope with disappointment. So, they face away from their counterparts. Anxiety raises the heartbeat. This is associated with the fact that they are not in a natural state of ease, which raises their alertness to internal and external uncertainties. They may have difficulty catching enough breath. Nervousness will be seen as trembling and sweating in the socially phobic.

Some experience stomach upsets and nausea, dizziness, light-headedness and mental emptiness. These symptoms characterize the socially phobic as one who does not experience life as it really is but exist in another 'cloudy atmosphere' that seems like not the natural one we know here on earth. Some develop abnormal eating habits – either overeating or underfeeding, or preference for certain foods over others or even addictions. They might also experience unusual muscle tensions whose causes may not be medically founded. It will be important to mention at this point that social phobia like overthinking, leads one into inactivity and inaction. They do not exercise their faculties and capabilities thereof. This could explain how it can lead to physical health issues.

Socially phobic individuals generally tend to avoid everyday events like meeting and interacting with unfamiliar people, attending social or family gatherings or parties, going to school or to work, initiating conversations, eye contact, eating in front of other people, using public washrooms, entering a room in which people are already seated, dating etc. if left untreated for long, social anxiety can lead to low self-esteem, passiveness is life, negative self-talk, poor social skills, hypersensitivity to criticism, low academic and life performance, drug and substance abuse or other forms of abuse, withdrawal from social circles and relationships and poor skills.

Image for communication

Social anxiety negatively impacts on self-confidence in the way that the victim does not go out to learn life skills or use them in practical ways. They develop doubt in the endowments and capabilities to perform simple tasks as well as face challenges that may come their way. When one gets to a point where the normal things that people do seem too big and difficult to comprehend and do, then they associate their incapability with their worth, as low, insignificant or inconsequential. They also develop the belief that they are mentally incompetent compared to their peers and generally stay away from responsibility.

Controlling Fear

Do not tell everyone

You do not have to tell people that you are a person. Your close associates already know about it and have a way of accepting and dealing with your plight positively and constructively. The rest of the world have no idea about your shyness and have no interest and business with it. So, with respect to your shyness, ignore them. Your anxiety is not visible or amplitied as you think.

Take yourself lightly

Your friends will once every regular while bringing up the topic of your shyness right before you. Do not take it so seriously or personal. They are likely trying to sensitize you to overcome it. And the best way to start is to talk about it casually to keeping your tone light and friendly. Do laugh about it. Speak too about it light-heartedly. It truly does not hurt. It helps.

Have your tone of soundness

You are bound to blush in some situations. You might sometimes want to fidget. But trust your mental soundness and keep it clearly above your displays of weakness or submission. Acknowledge the fact that you blushed and say that in a confident tone, to tell your audience or counterpart that you are not entirely the weakness they might have just seen when you blushed.

Know your entire individuality

You have so much more to tell and show about you. It is unlikely that you have never been good at something before. It is unlikely that you have never accomplished a goal before. It is unlikely that you have never face people and individuals before. However, you seem, you have made it here. And you came this far not because of the shyness trait and label on you but for all the other good traits that you possess. Define yourself on the basis of the sum of all your facultative strengths and endowments, rather than a single undermining trait and live up to your true identity.

Ignore your inner critic

Do not give in to the tendencies to cast yourself down into negative light in your own eyes. When you catch yourself nailing yourself down with negative self-statements, tell yourself to stop. Dwell on the thoughts that you have the innate and intrinsic power and skill to live your life in the positively.

Build your strengths

List down endowments and strengths that set you up for a life of activity and action. Learn, practice and master your skills and solving problems, creating new ideas and things and overcoming difficult moments. A conscious awareness of your gifts natural and acquired will remind you how much you have to offer to the world, and point you to a place of relevance, where you can prosper in your capabilities.

Make your relations wisely

Invest your time to find and make friendships and relationships with people who understand you for who you are with your strengths and limitations. Have your checklist against which you will determine the degree to which to interact with the people you relate within your life. Have good concern for the people who are warm, responsive and encouraging to you and your objectives. Give and receive your rewards in such associations with an open heart and mind, and you will surely open your chances of growth and prosperity.

Cease from your naysayers

Everyone has a group of people who will act with cruelty and sarcasm towards them, and you are no exception. Simply avoid them. Many who really do not care what you do with your life will not stop to think whether they are helping in advancing goodness. They will want to force you away from your good intentions and into their ill demands with the view to show you as incapable and inconsiderate. Always keep a healthy safe distance away from them.

Observe closely

Many people are dealing with themselves harshly thinking that they are the only ones who have made poor choices in life and are thus leading a regretful life. But with a little bit more interest to really observe how others lead their lives, you will notice how they also exhibit their signs of weakness and insecurity and how they could be suffering from that. You are not alone. But you can be better off if you took the relevant steps to free yourself of self-criticism and lead a freer life – wilfully and thoughtfully.

See the big picture

When a thing or two goes wrong about a situation, you do not need to blame it all on your bad spells. Your shyness mostly has nothing to do with what goes wrong. In every event, there are a number of players, each with their roles to play and contribute to the successful completion of it. It is not always your mistake. Also, the fact that something went wrong at the start does not mean it cannot get better with time. Similarly, minor negative events do not outdo the many positive things that happen. Know that the intended outcome of a process does not end up at one minor misguided event.

See yourself in a better light

The socially phobic normally has a negative image of themselves and bearing. You think you do not deserve much credit for anything because you are useless. You think you are irredeemable. But that is not true. People see you more positively than you actually think. They know you have greater potential. They know they owe you more respect. They are willing to sacrifice more for you. Think of yourself in this way too, and you will be readier to advance your course of growth and development as a person.

Belittle you fright

So, you are preparing for the forthcoming event or activity and are developing fear and anxiety as has been usual with you. Instead of freezing out at the thoughts of fears, stare the fears down and lean into them until they are no more. The decision you make to zoom in on dealing with your fears is critical for you to gain ownership and control of your plans and activities and that way ensures that all goes according to your intentions.

Deal with your fears

Create time every day to note down the worries and bothers that baffle your thoughts minds. Make a plan to settle each of those worries with a zeal and commitment at it every single day. Some can be silenced right away, while some can be addressed at the end of the day. There are others that simply require you to address them by evaluating your long-term plans and staying optimistic that your goals will come to pass when duly worked at in every possible necessary way.

Overcoming Social Anxiety

Challenge your negativity tendencies

Your default tendencies as a social phobic are to think that you have no control over your feelings and actions. But the truth is that you actually do not give thought. Begin to think that you can do something about your feelings and thoughts. Learn to question your feelings and thoughts as they arise and take note of what they really mean and whether it is beneficial for you to honour and act with them.

Practice mindfulness

Practising mindfulness is simply training yourself to be present when thinking, feeling and deciding on anything you want to do. Be present with yourself and aware of what you want to get out of imaginations and actions and be sure that you are actively and soberly going through the process with your full senses. Being mindful helps you not to judge yourself, but to understand and regulate yourself till you achieve your goal.

Take time out

The phobic tries to remain in familiar environments and do the same things over and over. But you can make an objective to try out new places leisurely. Instead of working from your house, trying to carry your laptop to the coffee shop and or to the park, etc. and work from there. Observe how people meet each other and converse there. The thought to expose yourself to the new relaxed environment will open up your social being and help you expand your receptiveness and social interests into a larger wider world.

Heal yourself beforehand

Identify some ten most dreadful situations in your social life and list them down in the increasing order of impact. Expose yourself to these events beginning with the least dreadful to the most dreadful. For instance, begin by just entering a dark room and staying there for a while before turning on the lights or walking out. Then walk on the streets and try saying hi to strangers. The objective is not to see how they will respond, but the fact that you overcame your fear and did something you initially dreaded. Repeat these actions until they become natural with you.

Focus on the activity or event

When preparing for an activity or event, focus on giving it all your attention so as to bring it out the best way you can. Do not think of your limitations at it, but what you have to put in and shape it out the best way possible to your abilities. Dress well for the event and walk into the interview knowing you did everything possible to make the event a success. Recognize, too, that everyone is concerned with the completion of the activity at hand, not with you. The more you focus on the task, the more composed you become and the more insight you gain and offer. That is what is needed for the start.

Match up your lifestyle

Know your foods, exercises, clothing, colours and hairdos, your, etc., read books, try new hobbies etc. Avoid foods that upset your moods. Giving adequate attention to yourself, your body, your mind, your outlook sets you up for positives actions and results. Optimism and positivity go with a positive outlook. Being tops with yourself, sets you top with the rest of the world.

Finally, be gentle with yourself and always remember to act confidently. A combination of all these factors will help your top face your fears.

Chapter 5

Self Confidence and Self Love

E veryone desires to be happy, fulfilled, and successful in what they do. However, this does not come on a platter of gold. There are many factors that come together to make this possible. One of which is self-confidence. This chapter is dedicated to shedding light on why you need to develop self-confidence. But before that, a little about self-confidence:

Self-confidence is having faith in yourself and your ability. It is faith in yourself to surmount any obstacle or challenge that faces you. It is self-confidence that keeps you on track when the going gets tough. It is the ingredient you need to forge ahead when everyone doubts your ability.

Self-confidence is not about being able to combat all challenges alone. It is also about having the wisdom to understand your restrictions and limitations as well as ways to make up for that.

How do you know a Confident Person?

When you have a goal and a passion, not everyone will share it. Also, the goal will not make sense to everyone as well. As a result of this, it is not uncommon for short-sighted people to criticize your effort. A confident person is smart enough to own up to mistakes and forges ahead, without worrying about what others think or feel.

Life throws us difficulties and challenges every step of the way, however, a confident person will rise above this. It is self confidence that will keep his resilience in the face of dangers and difficulties. A self-confident person is not afraid of making mistakes and learning from them as they know that no one is above mistakes. They are mentally strong are not bothered about others rising or doing well in their chosen field and career as they are not intimidated by the success of others. As a result of this, they willingly offer help to those who need it.

Why is Self Confidence Important?

As you go through life and all it throws at you, it is important to be able to keep your life in order and stay on track. In our quest for daily bread and our bid to pursue our passion, the ability to keep going is very important, despite all odds. Odds might come in, and from various angles which could be from people of authority, circumstances beyond our control, etc. It is self-confidence that will prevent you from being overwhelmed and outwitted.

All in all, self-confidence is a vital ingredient that is paramount to our success. This is why self-confidence is one of the main attributes of great leaders. It is not an attribute for leaders or top executives alone. If you are wondering why self-confidence is important, here are some cogent points why you must develop your self-confidence.

You get to Build Your Resilience

According to Friedrich Nietzsche, "What does not kill you makes you stronger."

This is a theory with the intention to prove that difficult times are not there to clip our wings. Besides, it takes courage and determination to face challenges that can "kill someone." As long as you are human, you are bound to face setbacks and failures, no matter your level of confidence. The place of self-confidence in this is the ability to handle these challenges and difficult situations such that you come out strong. Bear in mind that there are times things will not go as planned, but you can rise above the disappointments.

With time, with every obstacle you surmount, you will discover that mistakes and setbacks are all ingredients on your path of growth and success. With self-confidence, the fear of failure is out of the way. With this, breaking new grounds and stretching yourself does not scare you as you are confident in your ability to rise against all the odds.

Self Confidence helps you get what you Want

There is a way self-confident people carry themselves is such that everything about them reflects it. In a discussion, for instance, a speaker who engages the audience by distributing eye contact evenly in the room and makes the audience part of the discussion will come across as confident. This is in contrast to a presenter who looks down throughout the presentation and avoids the audience's gaze.

A self-confident person is not afraid of expressing himself to get what he wants. This is different from being arrogant. This is because self-confidence helps you engage others, ask the right questions for you to get what you want. In other words, you know how to play your cards right, without using other people to achieve your goals. This explains why an employer would rather hire a candidate that displays confidence in an interview, compared to another, irrespective of his brilliance. A brilliant person, without self-confidence, might even find it difficult to express himself articulately to get what he wants.

Self Confidence Fuels Your Dream

Many people have the ideal life they have always wanted in their mind. However, they discover that they cannot seem to make it a reality. Many times, what such people lack is confident to go after what they want. Being self-confident does not mean life will be rosy, and you will have all you need to accomplish what you aim for. However, with confidence comes the assurance that you can accomplish what you set out to.

As discussed in the opening paragraph, self-confidence gives you the guts to go after something, even though many others lack faith in you. Among other things, it is what will keep you going, ensuring that you stay true to the task, against all the odds.

You get to have Improved Relationships

One of the attributes of less confident people is that they become less focus and obsessed with themselves. I have been there before. There were periods when I was bothered about the opinions of others and needed their validation. I walked with the consciousness that people were constantly evaluating me and carefully scrutinizing my words, in case I said something stupid.

The reality, however, is that this is not always true. People are more caught up in their own life, challenges, and worries to be scrutinizing another person. Hence, when you improve your self-confidence, you will build better relationships and interactions because you will not worry so much of what people think of you. This will keep you relaxed and focused on building better relationships.

You get to make the right Decisions

One of the attributes people without adequate self-confidence is their tendency to want to please others. They act to please others, rather than do what they want. As a result of this, they are prone to making the wrong decisions.

Self-confident people, on the other hand, make decisions that go alongside their wishes, desires, and goals. They are passionate about what drives them and expect others to see and believe in their dreams and visions, rather than living life to please others, which affect the type of decisions they make.

Self Confidence Fosters Productivity

Many of the points we have discussed above points to the fact that self-confidence boosts productivity. With self-confidence, you get to pursue your dream, go after what you want with zeal and determination, and build resilience. Together, these traits help improve your productivity.

Lack of or inadequate self-confidence, on the other hand, has a way of making you focus on the task that will work against your productivity. You find yourself doing things to pass some time. This, in turn, prevents you from focusing on what can make you productive. Being confident in your abilities, on the other hand, will make you productive.

The Relevance of Self-Love

If there is an important lesson you need to learn, a lesson you need to sink into your consciousness, it is that you are the most important person in the universe. I do not know how many years you have lived on this planet, but you have survived all odds, and you are still standing. You have risen against the tides as well as everything life threw at you.

If you consider yourself in relation to the entire universe, you might just be another being. But in your world, you are very important, you matter!

In improving your social skills and developing self-confidence, the importance of loving yourself cannot be overemphasized. It is one of the best things you can do for yourself. The previous section talks about self-confidence. However, you need to know that loving yourself is part of the recipe for developing self-confidence.

Loving yourself is the secret to a happy and content life. When you are at peace with yourself, it will reflect in the ways you behave and relate to others, hence reflecting on your social skill, the overall theme of this manual. There is so much about loving yourself that it is the key to a carefree life, a life void of worry and unhealthy comparison that might shoot down your confidence and social skills.

It is, however, to note self-love does not come on a platter of gold. In fact, one of the reasons many people struggle with social skills is due to their lack of belief in themselves and their attitude. This is not surprising as man, by nature, is wired to be his biggest critic.

Thanks to Mother Nature, we tend to be harder on ourselves than we are on others. With time, as this self-hatred progress, it bites deep into various parts of our life. This attitude gradually lowers our confidence level, steals our self-esteem, and the result is glaring — poor social skills.

This is why loving yourself is one of the most important things you can do to boost your self-confidence and in turn, improve your social skills. Now here comes the question: How can you love yourself? There are many things you can do to develop self-love. However, we have handpicked the critical ones which you can apply, and you are guaranteed to see a significant improvement in your life.

Have Time to Yourself

By having time for yourself, we mean having time to do what you love. It could be a few days set apart in a month or a few hours in a day. With this, you get comfortable with yourself and your company. This is one of the best ways to develop self-love.

Having time to yourself could mean going to the movie theatre, going on a date with yourself, cultivating a garden, trying something new. The idea is to spend time and get comfortable with yourself to develop your social skills.

Give Yourself a Break

It is natural for us to be hard on ourselves at times. We have set some unrealistic standard for ourselves, standards that we do not use for our friends and loved ones. No one is perfect; hence, there will be mistakes at times. When you do, learn from your mistakes, pick yourself up, and move on.

Being too hard on yourself for your mistakes will have some negative psychological effects on you. This will affect your self-confidence and your ability to improve your social skills.

Say No to Others Without Feeling Guilty

One of the things that sets self-confident people apart is the ability to live their lives without worrying so much about the approval of others. Pleasing others is not in their dictionary, unlike people who lack self-love. Lack of self-love is seen in the way people bend over backwards to please others and get on their good side. However, the ability to respectfully say no to others when necessary is essential to foster self-love.

Have a List of Your Accomplishments

This is not about being proud; it is about having pride in yourself and your abilities to make things happen for yourself. At times, the motivation you need to keep going is found from within. In other words, looking back at how far you have come can rekindle some hope in yourself and your ability. The satisfaction and hope from what you have been able to achieve could be the torch needed to see the tremendous potential hidden in you.

Without obnoxiously tooting your own horn, feel free to let others know your accomplishment without feeling guilty. Be proud of what you have achieved and give yourself credit for it.

Let Go of dark past and Hurts

No one is perfect, and the fact that you are human already qualifies you for mistakes and errors. Some errors are simple to forget while others linger on. The weight from this past error could hold you down and prevent you from living life to the fullest, hence hurting your progress and affecting the relationship you have with yourself. and hurt your progress.

You have to realize that everyone has a questionable past; hence, you have to stop being hard on yourself. This only makes you a human being, not a bad person. With this in mind, you have to let go of the dark past that has been holding you down to develop a love for yourself.

Stay Away from people that bring you down

In other words, know your worth. You are better off without some relationships. Individuals who do not add value to your life or disregard your value is not worth it. Being around those who bring you down will diminish your self-worth and affect your social skills.

The people who are worth being friends with should be those who inspire, motivate, and drive you to success. They should support and keep you going despite all odds.

Make the Necessary Changes in Your Life

The only thing constant in life is change. Besides, bear in mind that there is neither anyone nor anything that can keep you happy for life. If people can keep themselves happy for a long time, the rate of divorce would not be so high. The point here is that you need to get comfortable with doing what you have not done before. The experience that comes from attempting new things is enough to help you develop the kind of love and motivation you need to keep going.

Be Grateful for what You Have

By now, we have realized that things will not always go our way. However, learning to accept what life throws at you graciously is one of the keys to being happy and content with your life.

Besides, many people desire to be where you are. While you might not have a say at the what life throws at you, you are in control of the way you react. Hence, choosing to be grateful for what you have will help you develop self-love.

Chapter 6

Exercises You Can Do to Improve Your Social Skills

H ere are some highly useful tricks and exercises you can try in your free time to help you get closer to your goal of achieving greater charisma.

While a total shift of attitude: from negative to positive, unsure to confident, greedy to grateful, out of focus to present takes time and a steady amount of determination and energy, exercises can help you fine-tune and hone your skills to really shine when you need to the most.

1. Exercise to Build Rapport

Humans are largely emotion-driven beings. Very few of us use logic to guide us. When conveying charisma and confidence, you will not be successful unless people trust you. This is the essence of rapport.

Do this exercise with someone don't yet know. This may seem daunting, even scary, but they will not know it is an exercise—only you will. What is even better is that you are going to do the exercise in a low-pressure environment, such as the grocery store. This is going to take you to task regarding building instant rapport. If it does not work out the first time, try it again!

The meaning of genuine connection is hard to put into words, but it is the same way we instantly know if something is inappropriate or even obscene—it is an instinctive, almost primal reaction. When you experience a genuine connection with someone, these are a few of the signs you will be looking for:

- a sudden, genuine smile or laughter that is mirrored in the eyes
- the sharing of a personal fact, feeling, or story
- the other person letting their guard down

When you are caught in a moment with someone else—and by caught I mean you are both in the same moment by coincidence, and cannot leave that moment, such as in a checkout line at a store, in an elevator, waiting at an airport gate, or on public transport—try to make brief conversation with them. This is much easier with someone who is the employee in a situation where you are the customer, of course. You can ask them how their shift is going, how life is treating them, or what they think of a product you are buying.

In a situation such as an elevator, choosing a non-invasive question or topic is important, especially if you are male and the only other person is a woman. For the purpose of this exercise in those situations, it is best to wait for another opportunity, as women are frequently on their guard around men they do not know, for obvious reasons. We do not want to make someone afraid or uncomfortable for the sake of an exercise.

However, if the person you're with is obviously happy (if they're smiling, for instance) you can ask them, "What's your secret to being in a great mood?" Make sure you are smiling as well so that you are not accidentally misunderstood as being sarcastic.

Look for some component of their answer that will help you create a conversation. Say for instance they answer, "I just like to be cheerful. My mom raised me to always look on the bright side," you can say, "That is a good way to look at life. Where were you raised?"

They might answer with "Maine. I'm going back home to visit in a month, I can't wait!"

When someone shares something personal such as this, then you know you have scored a win in the rapport exercise.

2. Exercises to Instantly Reduce Stress

Why do I need to reduce stress, in the middle of a book about improving my charisma? You might ask. The reasoning behind this is that we all carry stress, visibly, in our bodies, in our faces, and in our eyes. Other people can sense it from a mile away, and while happiness is contagious, so is anxiety and stress. We might not even realize we are holding on to stress, it is just that natural. However, if we learn instant tricks to let it go, we can shift that stress right out of our bodies before walking through a door to a party, date, meeting, or interview.

The breath in calm, breathe out stress technique: Breathe is extraordinarily powerful. We need it to live and we breathe thousands of times a day without focusing on it or controlling it. When we choose to control it, however, breathe can be an effective tool to use in calming the mind and relaxing the body. Think about when you are at the doctor's for a simple checkup and she asks you to breathe so she can listen to your heartbeat. Unless we are feeling ill or out of sorts, this moment almost instantly calms us down, right?

In the cab, your car, the elevator, the lobby of the building—anywhere that you can do a series of slow, deep breaths without someone giving you the side-eye—breathe in through your nose, deeply. You will know you have taken in enough breathe when your stomach pushes out, and always remember to keep your shoulders still. Healthy, natural breathing has everything to do with your diaphragm and nothing to do with your shoulders.

Hold the breath for half a second. Imagine the fresh air you have just taken in surrounding and latching onto the stress in your body, then exhale through your nostrils and imagine the stress leaving your body, never to return. Do this again and feel the stress in your hands be pulled out of your body. Do it one more time, and this time imagine the stress leaving your face.

Facial exercise: Our faces can be exhausted, especially when we deal with other people all day long. Refresh your facial muscles by taking a moment in private (you can do this in front of the bathroom mirror at work or in a restaurant if you're not at home, or even in a bathroom stall), and moving your face in as many different positions as you can. It is going to look very silly when you do, but it works! Actors often do this before the director begins to shoot a scene, just to "reset" their face and deliver believable facial expressions.

3. The Instant Focal Shift

When entering a room, an instant rapport and charisma boost is to immediately shift your point of focus away from yourself and towards the others in the room. People notice when someone is giving them their full attention, and they respond positively to that. They also respond immediately to someone who seems to be distracted, disinterested, or caught up within themselves—and the response is not a good one.

This is something many of us fail to consider when we walk into a meeting or interview. We are primarily focused on a) getting there, b) finding a place to sit, and c) gathering our thoughts together. In order to make an excellent impression, you need to get your thoughts together before you enter that room. Then, when you do walk through the door, acknowledge everyone in the room with your eyes. Try a genuine smile when you make eye contact with someone. Once you've acknowledged everyone, that is when you can look for a seat—usually, someone will pull out a chair or guide you to a seat that's empty, which is a great opportunity to start things out with a "Thank you."

Focusing your attention on to other people instead of yourself has the added benefit of moving your mind away from any nervousness, insecurities, or bad habits you might have—when you stop focusing on yourself, it is easier to project confidence, rather than exude anxiety.

4. Try a Powerful Pose

One of the fastest ways to hack the human brain and cause an inner upswing of confidence is through body language. A Harvard professor performed a study where volunteers were asked to assume poses of confidence and poses of insecurity. When the volunteers posed confidently, their levels of cortisol, the hormone produced during times of stress, dropped, and their testosterone levels rose. The insecure poses had the opposite effect.

Want an instant confidence boost? Here are some physical poses to do to instantly raise confidence chemically in your brain:

- At your desk, lean comfortably back in your chair with your feet up, and then fold your hands behind your head.

- Stand facing a table and lean forward to rest your weight on your hands—keep your palms down on the table's surface.

- Stand tall, feet apart, with your hands on your hips.

- Sit in your chair, and then lean back. Cross one leg over the other leg's knee, resting your ankle on your knee. Again, hands are held behind your head, crossed and cradling it.

- Sit in your chair with your legs apart, and rest your arm across the back of an empty chair next to you.

5. Ask a Friend to Become Your Charisma Partner

So many of us are hesitant, even loathe asking for help when it comes to feelings and emotions. Confidence is a feeling—and at first, when you are just learning to become more charismatic, it may be as easy to lose confidence, as it is to gain it. Again, there should be no shame in this. Shame is a useless emotion and will only hold you back. By reaching out for help, you are showing, proving, that you are a strong person who knows when they need some assistance. Strong people solve problems—weaker people ignore their problems because of their egos or their pride.

When your confidence is flagging, reach out to a trusted friend for help. Studies show that people who receive a boost from friends or peers enjoy long-term healing effects from such a connection, which in turn boosts their overall confidence. Conversely, you can be their lifeline when your friend needs help with their own confidence.

6. Use Music to Pump You Up

Music is an incredibly powerful tool when we want to give our brains a boost. Music can help the workday go by faster, can help a trip become more memorable, can connect us in large groups, and it allows us to tap into our deeper emotions. By listening to a high-energy song, your serotonin and endorphin levels will naturally increase, your tension will lessen, and your confidence will rocket skyward. Studies have discovered that songs with a heavier bassline work the best in pumping us up—think of rock anthems or stadium dance songs. Make a short playlist that can become a go-to on days you need some help with confidence.

7. Adopt an Alter-Persona

At first, you may think, wait, seriously? Pretend to be someone I am not? Sort of, but actually, we are talking about being a different version of you. Celebrities, performers, and even mixed martial artists and professional wrestlers do this. It is okay to have different sides of yourself—that is very natural. So consider cultivating the "big energy" version of yourself when you need a confidence pick-me-up.

One of the easiest ways to practice this energy-shift is to imagine a charismatic, powerful and present character, then be that character during your next work-related phone call. Ask yourself what would this character choose to do, what they would they sound like, and say?

After a while, you are going to develop and utilize your own Charisma-based skill set, but playing a role in the interim can help you adopt some of your alter ego's techniques and style.

8. Refuse to Allow a Less-Than-Awesome Self Image

This is such a widely overlooked problem that it is often the last thing we think about, although it should be our first! What is your self-image like? When you leave the house to conquer your day, do you feel just a little bit like an imposter? If your outer shell does not match your inner core, it is going to show. We want to come across as present, authentic, warm, and real. How can we do that if instead, our self-image is afraid, indisposed, unsure, and distorted?

Take some time to look inward. Be honest about what you see. Do you feel good about the image of you that you are imagining? If not, then it is time to take some steps:

- When you picture yourself, first picture your body. This may be uncomfortable for those of us with body-related hang-ups, such as our weight, our physique, our height, or an area of the body that we are self-conscious about. Next, imagine if a graphic artist used Photoshop to make you look better. See that improved image in your mind. This is not to allow you to feel bad about your current body. We have all seen living, breathing, examples of people with our exact same body type who we have thought looked terrific—this phenomenon happens all the time! The problem arises when we cannot feel how those people look—the issue is not a physical one, it is an emotional one. So use that inner graphic designer ASAP. Now, every time you imagine how you look, see that improved image—soon you will emanate that and project it. That is how others will see you.

- Beyond your physical persona, how do you see your attitude, your personal power, and your energy? If you see it all over the place or lagging, you can improve that as well, using your mind to re-draw that person you see. Imagine yourself confident, winning, being charismatic with others. Refuse to see the former image—the new image is your reality.

- Kick the negative thoughts right out of your head. This is serious! We discussed this earlier but it is essential to that better self-image that you follow through. The instant a negative thought pushes its way into your head, boot it out! Do not let it linger for a minute. You do not have the time or energy for that. Always...think...positive thoughts! An example: many of us have these instant reactions to frustrating problems: "This is too difficult" and "I can't," or "this is a bad day." Those are all self-defeating. They will literally make the situation harder for you. Pronouncing a day as "bad" will ensure that it is bad. Why settle for that when you have the power to change things with mere thoughts and words? Instead of "this is too difficult," say "I've got this" or "I can do this"--then give yourself the time you need to think it through, try different approaches, and get it done, and never be afraid to ask for help. Rather than saying "I can't," say "I will figure out a way." Instead of saying "this is a bad day," give yourself permission to say "this is a challenging day," and consider admitting that "I'll probably learn a lot from today."

- Learn about who you are. If you do not know yourself then you will be ill equipped to defeat your own bad habits and thoughts. Knowing ourselves means learning about both the good and the bad. Once we do, we can utilize our strength and wisdom to change that bad to good.

- Be a person of action. Acting in a positive way will activate all the other areas of yourself, and trigger them to be positive as well. Positivity is essential to success when it comes to charisma and confidence. People become what they choose to do. Your choices build the future you, day by day. If you choose to live positively, you will become more positive, it is as simple as that.

- Choose to be kind and generous. You might think this is a little too hokey, but studies prove that when people choose to be kind, they grow more powerful. A kind act provides an instant surge in empathy and presence, which in turn, activates our charisma. Being generous taps into your feelings concerning abundance and gratitude. Choose to act with kindness and generosity when you can; soon, you will be hooked on the positive feelings and feedback that comes from living this way.

- Become a lifelong student. Take time each day to practice something you want to be competent in; study things you want to retain. When you raise your competence level, it naturally transfers into your confidence.

- Slow your speech down. Not too slow, but not fast, either. People who speak too quickly are doing so because they are afraid they are going to run out of time, or the other person's attention, or both. When you speak with purpose, you command attention. Not in a forceful way, but in a way that shows you are speaking from a place of inner conviction and strength.

- Build your confidence by setting small, realistic goals, then achieving them. By doing this, you are proving to yourself that you are capable of achievement.

- Get rid of bad habits, one (small) habit at a time. Getting in the practice of both noticing your bad habits, and conquering them, will give you the confidence you need to tackle bigger habits that need to change. Try waking up a few minutes earlier each day or walking an extra 15 minutes when you go out to exercise.

- Be a solution-based person. If your point of view tends to settle on the problems, such as "Okay I see what the problem is, it's (you describe the problem and stop there)," then it is time to shift focus and become the person who has an idea of how to solve the problem. Don't let the sentence end with the problem, instead, say "We can see that this is the problem, and I think doing (a, b, or c) is a way that we can try to solve it." When it comes to personal issues, take negative thoughts such as "I always procrastinate" and turn them around, instead of saying "How can I learn to stop putting things off?" Then focus on the solution.

- Choose to volunteer in some capacity. This goes back to the being generous and kind, but it takes it a step further in that you're going to be around people who are unfamiliar to you (at first). This brings together the importance of generosity with the opportunity to practice your charisma skills.

9. Become an Intuitive Communicator

When someone is speaking to you, there are important techniques you should use. First, never try to anticipate their words or finish their sentences. Even if you know, where their point is going, let it go there—this is their story to tell and you are showing them respect when you give them room to tell it in. Be present while listening—do not let your mind wander off to start formulating a response because you have not heard the whole point yet. Remember, charisma takes work, and being a good listener involves an investment of time and patience.

- When the person is finished, wait a moment before responding. It can be helpful to ask them clarifying questions, or repeating back certain things they stated, adding a "is that correct?" to make sure they know you listened to them. If you respond immediately after they stop talking, they are going to know that you were not really listening, but instead just waiting for your turn to speak, which is the opposite of empathic and charismatic, as well as disrespectful.

10. Work on Your Body, and Gain a Happier Mind

This may seem obvious, but many people fail to realize the immediate impact any kind of physical activity has on the mind and positive hormone levels in the brain. Often, we ignore our body throughout the workday and are just too tired to do anything physical once we return home. The simple fact is there is always time for exercise breaks, we just overlook them.

If you work for 40 minutes, then take a 5-minute break to stretch or lift free weights standing by your desk, in an 8-hour day you will have accomplished a decently sized workout.

Movement, strength-building exercise, cardiovascular activities, and toning exercises all serve to support our charisma-building agenda of positive thinking, better posture, inner strength, and gratitude. Do not ignore your body if you want to cultivate a more confident mind.

11. Refuse to Engage In Negative Conversation

One of the easiest ways to get people talking is to complain about something, however, you will notice that if you do, the only people you have caught the attention of are the negative folks. This is too easy, so do not fall for it—refuse to begin conversations by pointing out the negative aspect of something.

Case in point: a father and son were standing in a long line at a Salvation Army store. The only cashier was patiently ringing up a full shopping cart worth of garments for a Native American woman. While this was happening, the man in front of the father and son was growing increasingly impatient: sighing loudly and looking around for someone to connect within anger. The father refused to meet the other man's gaze, instead of looking out over the racks of clothes beyond his son.

The woman checking out realized she would need her husband's credit card, and that he was waiting in the car for her. She apologized and left the store to retrieve it. The line of customers waiting was respectfully silent, but the man in front of the father and son finally voiced his opinion that "That is the most annoying customer I've ever seen in my life."

This time, the father allowed the man to make eye contact with him.

The father said, "You know, businesses like these assists many folks. If someone wants to spend a lot of money here, I imagine that could only be helpful to the charity itself."

The angry man replied, "I am allowed to have opinions. This is America."

The father nodded, and said, "That is true. And she was here first."

Nobody else spoke, but everyone else was listening. Whom do you think the rest of the customers empathized with the most in this conversation? Perhaps some had sided with the angry man, but the father made a better impression.

12. The Importance of Boundaries

When navigating the social and business world, it is essential that we know our own personal boundaries, and are prepared to defend them. Being charismatic does not mean being a pushover. There is a fine line to walk between charm and acquiescence. A confident person does not sit idly by while someone else marches all over his or her personal space, ideals, ethics and values, and self-respect.

If you are starting your own business or have just landed a work-heavy new promotion, you might be tempted to forego all personal time or pleasure and just dive in, headfirst. The trouble is you are on a fast track to exhaustion. You need to learn to delegate; you also need how to say no, in a secure, non-threatening manner.

When framing a decline, state it simply and do not pile on the excuses why you are not able to perform what has been asked of you at this time. Offer an alternative solution that is in everyone's best interests.

13. Don't Live For Validation from Others

It is important to win the respect of other people, but at the end of the day, nothing you do should be solely for the purpose of others' validation. You need to foster self-respect and a feeling of accomplishment. Those things come from within, not from the words of other people.

14. Don't Be Afraid to Become Passionate

Getting passionate about something lights a fire within you that others can see and admire. Do not be afraid to let yourself show what truly excites and motivates you in life. Hiding creates the opposite effect of being charismatic.

15. Be True to Yourself

Finally, everything that you do should contain a reflection of who you are as a person. There are always more choices and opportunities. Do not live your life chasing someone else's dream; cultivate your own goals and dreams, then go after them. No one has the right to dictate how anyone lives his or her life. Life is an exciting journey, with reveals and hidden knowledge just for you—get out there and explore what intrigues you the most.

Chapter 7

Conversation And Tips For Improving Conversation

Starting a Conversation

It is obvious that a conversation starts at a point and therefore there is a point at which it should also come to an end. This is because making a conversation too long can create discomfort and sometimes points to insensitivity. When a conversation is flowing well and both of you seem immersed in it should not mean that you keep going on and on.

This is particularly if you are the one who initiated the conversation. If the other person opened up to you and gave you room to converse with them, they are probably trusting that you know the proper timing to end the conversation.

There are people who are giving the courtesy by accepting to go on with the conversation. But they could be sending signals about wanting to leave it at that. The possible care that it will be rude to just pull out the conversation when you seem to be keeping it rolling.

Opportune Time to End

When you are conversing with someone you just met, you will be helping yourself to keep the conversation relatively brief. The briefness depends on the conversation and the level of engagement between the two of you. You should be able to judge that by your intuition. The danger in keeping a conversation stretched is you both start to notice certain awkward moments. There comes in some form of strain on both of you.

When a conversation starts to have some strain, it becomes uncomfortable and it can feel forced. The other person who is stranger can start feeling bored and since they still have power over you, if you approached them, they probably will not think well of you. And ending the conversation beyond the ideal time becomes even difficult and may create an opportunity for the other person to show negativity towards you.

However, conversations can also feel awkward when they are brought to an end too quickly. This happens particularly with people who have anxiety over social interactions. When one has too much anxiety, they feel tension when there is a moment of silence comes about. They doubt themselves and perceive the danger of losing control of the situation. They then opt to bring the conversation to an end that could be abrupt and unexpected by the other party.

In this case, the other person starts to be caution in the future when they encounter you. This is particularly if they perceive they are some kind of threat and they make you uncomfortable. They want to hurry and go and hence it kills future conversations. When you end a conversation unexpectedly the other person feels awkward and questioning why they gave you attention in the first place.

When it is someone familiar such as a partner or friend abruptly ending a conversation can indicate that you lost your cool. They may also feel you are sensitive about the subject of the conversation and this may start to reduce the richness of the spectrum of your conversations. It can even start to change the fun in the way you relate with the other person.

Conversations should be brought to an end timely. This is when both of the people conversing have expressed themselves well. Having nothing more to be said means that it is time to bring the conversation to an end. Do not try to extend it r introduce a new subject as there will be a disconnection in the flow of the subject. Usually, a conversation that has to go on just switches to a new subject without the knowledge of those talking. You only realize later that you lost the ori8gnal subject of the discussion. However, when there is a clear show that everything has been said, it is a signal of concluding the conversation.

Make an Impression that Is Positive as You Close

Sometimes pauses naturally creep in when a conversation is switching topics and when the general tone of the conversation is changing. These poses that are necessitating a change of the mood or topic are the perfect timing to close the conversation. Signal that it is time to check out of the interaction and take an active role at this. You could do this by saying you like what the other person has said and how they are insightful.

It is about being gracious and warm, and showing that the conversation has been important because of the insights that the other person shared. For instance, intimate that "I am going to be thinking about how you described the food at the hotel. You are fun." This is a show that you paid attention to what that person was saying and that makes the conversation feel worthwhile. It is a conclusive signal while validating the other's role in the conversation which means that you found them refreshing.

When, for instance, you are talking about a certain event that is a current affair show that you have been enlightened. You could compliment the other person for their knowledge about it saying they are probably the best people to listen to on that matter. Say you are actually heading over to check out the article they mention in the paper. This signals the end of the conversation but showing you are not dismissive.

Once you are clear with your signal to bring the conversation to a conclusion, come up indicate that you look forward to meeting again. Plan on seeing the person again in order for them to be aware of you. If it is a stranger, suggest that you could arrange for a sit-down with them and familiarize themselves. Be specific about the day and time and let them suggest a different time. However, do not say you would like to see them sometime or to go out with them in the future. This in itself means that it will not happen.

If it is someone familiar, wind up by saying you will keep in touch. Say that you will call them. If it is someone that you are bound to meet later, tell them, "I'm going to see you tonight, right?" This ends the current conversation while starting to build the expectation for the meeting to come. It is about reinforcing the connection that is existing even as you part. Let them not feel as if ending the conversation means you are not interested. It could be that you need to get somewhere. It could also be releasing them to go if they send a signal to want the conversation. However, you are not just going to tell them to go.

However, it is not good to keep the parting moment drag on too long. Be on point and express what your feeling is about the conversation and deploy a body language that conveys the same message. Tell them goodbye mentioning their name as well to keep them alert. This could be a handshake, a smile and signaling eye contact. Then make the move to get going in order to avoid being ambiguous and overdoing things.

How to Dodge Conversations That are Problematic

In some instances, you can initiate a conversation and it soon takes a turn to the worse as opposed to better. This can be weighing heavily on you and you feel the conversation should be halted. There are times when a conversation is talking about a sensitive matter or is too aggressive than you could have it. You need to either get out of the conversation or simply halt it without making those involved feel offended or appearing a contemptuous person.

Conversations that have become too argumentative can be consuming and exhaustive and draw the worst out of you when you get carried away. The case is the same when you find yourself in the enmeshed in a conversation with a snob who is bragging about his qualities and exploits the whole time that you feel the conversation is suffocating you.

One way is to wait for the moment when they are pausing between sentences and fix a question or a series of questions. The yes/no questions work best in these situations as they can disrupt the follow of thought of the person. Once you successfully affect the questioning you gain the conversational ball that hands you the right to direct it. After realizing they are paying attention to you, at least for now, appreciate the last few things he said and congratulate the person for sharing their thoughts. Wish them well and notify them that you need to catch up with some friend on the other side of the lobby. Let them excuse you and shake hands with them as you smile and getaway.

This could sometimes make the other person realize how good you are and rethink their own ay of engaging you. It may surprise you when the next time they ask you if you were offended by something to which you say no. Some may realize how overwhelming they were and just get straight to apologize if that was too much for you to handle. Sometimes, getting out of certain conversations in the best way possible and at the most opportune time could be the thing that gets friendship rolling.

Handling the Kind That Is Always Complaining

There are people who think anyone who they meet is supposed to hear the adversity that is in their life only. They have all the positives to say about you and all the negatives to say about themselves. Sometimes they talk as if the positives they are noting about you are only making their problems worse. These are sympathy solicitors that want to control you by appealing to your emotions and triggering your soft spots.

It is never fun to meet someone who wants to make you responsible for their problems or to make you share them. It can just be as overwhelming as interacting with a braggart who wants to dominate you with egotism. They are suffocating and can make you have to resign to listen to things that have very little to do with you. This is not to mean you are not pitiful but that you are interacting and everyone has their issues in life. They probably also need some social skills just as much as you are trying to learn and practice execute. They have to know how to interact with people who are not at first are not related to their life and what is going on it.

You will have to handle this kind with a similar process of questioning them with yes or no questions. This makes them think you are starting to get concerned and it switches them off for a moment. Send some sentiments of sympathy for their predicaments in order to make sure they know you listened to them. It can be fine to even express your thoughts of concern through some advice that is unsolicited and which you do not care if they will matter. This should be shot and easy to understand. Avoid being thoughtful as you advise.

These could be telling them to keep trying, to hang in there and telling them that their way is for them to be hopeful. Tell them that it always works in the end. Tell them, you have to proceed to catch up with a friend. Call out their names as you say goodbye to them. They possibly will have no chance of finding the flow to keep telling about their problems and you quickly will have gotten out of such an undesirable situation.

Conversational Cues

Okay, everything seems to be going great. You are talking, people seem interested in you and your opinions, and the conversation is alive. They laugh at your jokes and comments, and they always keep in touch with you whenever there is a party coming up or any kind of social gathering that you might enjoy. That's great! So you decide to take the very same steps with another new group, and suddenly, it doesn't work. People feel a bit overwhelmed by your presence, or they don't pay attention like the first group did. What happened? You did exactly what you did before, and they responded differently. Where did you go wrong?

Well, the obvious answer is that you probably didn't do anything wrong. People respond differently to the same stimulation (that's the best part of society), and we must adapt accordingly. We talked about how we don't act the same way in front of our bosses as we do in front of our families and we adapt our attitude and approach of talking in an unconscious way. However, sometimes, we do things or act in ways that people who don't know us may not like. The best way to see if you are doing something that might be interpreted as an offence is to follow this guide.

Signs and conversational cues

1- Personal Space

Have you ever been in a conversation where one of the people involved is way too close to the other, almost like they were over them? This is what invasion of personal space looks like. If you are standing too close to someone, people won't care about what you are saying, because it is an intimidation tactic that is often used to overpower someone, since you are using your entire body to express your idea. This is entirely wrong, and it is something that should be avoided at all costs. In the same vein, if you are standing too far, your interlocutor won't be able to hear you correctly or give you the attention you deserve.

The best way to tackle this is to try to maintain a distance of three or four feet, and this depends on how familiar you are with that person. If it is a first-time conversation, use the range that I mentioned. But if you are quite familiar with that person, or you have seen each other before, you can talk closer. Be aware of hugs and kisses on the cheeks. People from South America and parts of Europe are used to it, and if you don't like it or are not prepared, it can result in an awkward situation. If you are hugged and don't particularly like it, you can try to politely refuse and explain that you don't enjoy it. The person should understand that hugs and invasion of personal space aren't for everybody. Keep this in mind if you ever travel to South America or Spain.

2- Tone of voice

If you work in an office where there are hundreds of employees, you will encounter this problem at least twice a week. Some people don't listen to their voice to see if it is too loud. I met someone who grew up in a house where the custom was to speak loud, and this led to several problems when it was time to enter the real world, to the point that he had to go to speech therapy to see if there was any way to improve with this. While this particular case is a bit on the extreme side, you will see this happening every day. But what if you do it without even knowing?

If you are in doubt about your voice, try to record it saying anything; for example, read a paragraph from the book you are currently reading, and listen to it. Does it sound loud? If you are still in doubt, you can try to consult with a doctor. They will guide you and help you if you have any speech impediment or complication.

In a conversation, always pay attention not only to what your speaker is saying, but how and why they are speaking. These are as important as the message itself, and you can learn a lot about the message by watching the tone, inflection, pitch, volume and articulation of their speech. The last thing that you want as a speaker is to have listeners misinterpret your message because you raised your voice a little, or moved your hands in an aggressive way, as this will lead to confusion.

3- Vocal Register

As a corollary to the previous point, no matter how important the message is, the tone and vocal register are what people will remember from your speech. The most important thing in a conversation is to use the correct vocal register for the topic you are discussing. For example, if it is a happy situation or a friendly gathering, you don't want to use a lower voice because that expresses sadness. Try to use a higher register in your voice to express your happiness. In the same vein, if you are at a funeral or at a hospital, you want to use a lower register because that is what is suited to the place and situation.

4- Tone of your Text

This is something that you will have to learn the hard way. No matter how much you practice, you will eventually make a mistake. But the best way to check if you are doing it correctly is to read a message you have composed on email or text two or three times after you have composed it. Sometimes, you will realize that perhaps it wasn't the best way to express yourself, and you can change or adapt accordingly. For example, if you are writing an email to your boss using your company's address, always be formal and avoid every attempt at friendship. Keep it professional, and it will be appreciated. If, however, you have a bond with your boss, then you can talk to him in a friendly manner over texts or on the phone. Be professional in a work environment, and helpful outside of it. This way, you keep a safe distance between your work life and personal life.

If you are in doubt about the tone, try to read it for a friend, family, or someone you trust. This way, they can give you an outside perspective of the situation. If they offer a critique or ideas, be open to listening to them. That's why you are talking to them, after all.

5- Fidgeting

This is a social cue that we have ingrained thanks to Hollywood and TV shows. You know when someone is playing with their hair while they are listening to you? How many times have we seen people in movies flirting with this exact move?

No matter what pop culture says, the truth is that most people take it as a universal sign of discomfort. If you are talking to someone, like a new friend, for example, and they start playing with their hair or shifting their weight from one foot to the other, they might be uninterested in the conversation or might be feeling uneasy about the subject that you are talking about. In the same vein, if you want to express and show how confident you are, you have to be aware of your fidgeting, and try your best to cut that habit out. Fidgeting is also a way to express nervousness, and you don't want that. Of course, if you are feeling uncomfortable about the subject, you can always politely tell your interlocutor that you can change the topic. Or, if you don't feel comfortable saying it, you can always just change the conversation.

6- Wardrobe choices

My mother once told me that I should "dress for the job that I want, not for the one that I have". This is a great piece of advice because it works on many levels. Unconsciously, we are more prone to following and listening to the advice of someone who is well dressed than the one of someone who doesn't care about their appearance.

On the other hand, a great way to see if your coworker or someone close to you is having a really bad time is to check their clothes. If you see that they are untidy, aren't clean, or look like a truck went over them (metaphorically speaking), you can try to talk to them to see if there's something wrong. Perhaps they are waiting for someone to ask them, and that person could be you. Practice empathy and active listening, and keep your eyes and ears open for any sign of a problem. Sometimes, our body language says more than what we actually say with words.

Chapter 8

How Social Interactions Can Affect To Create New Friendships

No matter who your friends are, you owe it to them to be a friend who has great things to offer. As you probably have first-hand experience with, being friends with someone who does not value you or does not take the time to check-in with you can feel like you are involved with someone who is selfish. Toxic friendships are dangerous and upsetting, so don't be that type of friend. Know that friendships take work and effort to maintain. You cannot expect to make a bunch of new friends and keep them all by doing nothing in return. You need to be there for them, show them that you care about what is going on in their lives.

If you want to make sure that you are being the greatest friend possible consider these tips on keeping your friendships active:

- Spend Time Together on a Weekend: When you are able to hang out with someone on a day that is not filled with obligations, you will get the chance to do more of what you want to do. Sunday mornings are normally a great time to spend with people. They are relaxed and open to many possibilities. Ensure that you do not have any other plans that will cut your time short with this person. Have breakfast together, and stay as long as you both want. From here, you can decide what you'd like to do next. Be spontaneous! Consider both your interests so that you can engage in a fun activity that you will both enjoy.

• Become Comfortable with Silence: In friendship, especially those that are well-established, you shouldn't expect every single moment to be filled with conversation. Learn how to accept silence as a treasure. Be comfortable in these moments, and do not feel that you have to fill them just for the sake of filling them. Those who are comfortable with one another, in general, do not need filler conversation in order to maintain this comfort. It might take time to reach this point with your various friendships, but know that accepting silence is not a negative thing. It can provide you with moments of reflection that can be great for the friendship. You might realize how much you enjoy spending this time with one another.

• Reach Out When You Are in Need: Having fun within a friendship is a great feeling, but being able to count on someone when you are unhappy can also be just as great. Make sure that you are working toward confiding in your friends because they are there for you. Whether you need emotional coaching or physical support, you should be able to reach out to your friends when you are in need. This type of reciprocated support system is what will take your friendship to the next level. It can be easy to think of fun things to do, but helping one another in dire times will become even more of a learning experience.

• Make Time for Them: You might have a busy day ahead of you, but when your friend asks you if you can be there for them, you should try your best to be there. Much like romantic relationships, friendships can also come with some forms of sacrifice. You do these things because you care about these people, and the action should be coming from a place of love. Never make your friends feel guilty for the time that you decide to reserve for them. They are just as important and worthy of support as you are. Even if there is not a bad situation unfolding, being there for your friends in general shows that you are committed to the friendship. Anything that you make time for is something you consider important, and it can mean a lot when others see this.

• Share Your Ideas: Your friends can help you develop your ideas. When you are able to brainstorm with them, a creative way of thinking happens. This creativity can take you far by opening your mind to new ideas or inspiring you to seek out new opportunities. It is no secret that friendships can help you grow, and it is a sign of a great friendship when you are able to discuss ideas with one another. Even if your friend isn't doing anything other than listening to you, this might be the exact boost of confidence that you need to keep reaching for your goals.

• Create Together: Working together to create something can be a great way to build your friendship. While you do not need to become business partners, even creating a piece of art together can be a way for you to bond. The creation process is fun and exciting. It becomes even more interesting when you share this with someone that you enjoy spending time with. This process will allow the two of you to come together with your ideas and select the one that you would like to see through. Not only is this fun, but it can help you grow individually.

- Pay Attention to Details: When you first meet someone, you likely aren't going to know every single detail about them. This part comes after some time of getting to know one another. Having attention to detail is a great trait to express within a friendship. From remembering your friends' birthdays to their favorite colors, you will be able to show them how much you care by taking the time to retain these details. Do not consider any detail too large or too small; know that they are all equally important. These details are what make your friends who they are.

- Take a Trip Together: Going on a vacation with your friend is a fun way to bond. While a European vacation might not be realistic for your time and budget, you can still find ways to travel together. Taking a simple road trip together to a nearby town for the day can prove to be just as fun as a whole vacation. When you are exploring a new place together, you will both be at the same starting point. From deciding which route to take and where you'd like to stop for food, you will be coming together with your friend to make these decisions. This is a meaningful way to spend time with one another.

- Share Your Past: Maybe your friends weren't there in your past, but that does not mean that you need to keep this from them. Sharing your past is a way of showing your friends how much you trust them. As you know, your past has a lot to do with the person that you have become today. It provides people with a deeper understanding of why you are the way that you are. If you feel like sharing this with a friend, this is a great thing. It will strengthen your bond and allow for a better understanding of who you are.

These ideas are only meant to get you started with strengthening your friendships. The best ideas come from the heart. You know your friends best, so make sure that you think about different ways to spend time together that will benefit things that you both enjoy doing. The simple idea of trying something new together can be enough to replenish the friendship. Because you are going to be putting in the time and effort to try this new thing, your friend is going to see how committed you are to the friendship.

The best part about friendship is that there are no rules! As long as you are treating one another with kindness and respect, there is nothing that you absolutely must do in order to be considered a great friend. What matters most is that you both feel fulfilled within the friendship. If there ever comes a point where you do not feel that you are fully being appreciated, speak up. Your friend won't always realize that you feel this way, so it is better to talk about how you feel and be honest about it instead of holding onto these feelings passive-aggressively. Do not assume that your friend can read your mind. It is within this excellent communication that you will be able to work through anything together.

Know that some people require different types of friendships. Traditionally, a friendship involves speaking to one another often and making the time to see each other in person whenever possible. Some people want what are known as "low maintenance friendships." These are the types of friendships where you do not talk or hang out as often, but you still maintain a successful friendship. Much like your own social abilities, some people are only going to want friendship in small doses.

This is okay, as long as both parties are happy and understanding of the dynamic.

Beware of those friendships that drain you. The opposite of low maintenance, having a friend who demands to see you all the time and wants to talk 24/7 can become a bothersome person to have in your life. While it is nice to think that your friend values you so much, it can actually become hindering to you if your friend starts 'punishing' you for the time that you cannot devote to them. This can include giving you the cold shoulder or treating you poorly in general. Be on the lookout for friendships like these because this is an indication of toxicity.

How to Be You

It is easy to become lost in others' habits and mannerisms. While you feel that you might have the hang of socialization and friendship, know that staying true to who you are is still very important. Do not allow the opinions of others to completely take over your own morals and values. You are still your own person, no matter how many friends you acquire along the way. Remember, your true self is what got you these friends, to begin with. If you simply transform into someone else, people might begin to miss the original version of you that you presented them with.

The more time that you spend with someone, the more likely it is that you will pick up on their behaviors. This is something that happens naturally within friendships. Think about the person that you are closest to right now, no matter who it is. Chances are that you have some similarities in the way that you talk, think, and act. This doesn't have to be a bad thing, as long as you remember that you also have your own wonderful traits. Adopting traits from your friends can be great, as long as you do not completely take on their personality, too.

Spending some time to work on yourself will make you a better friend. Now that you have the ability to make friends and build connections, spending time alone is likely the last thing that you will want. Know that this will benefit all your friendships and future interactions, though. Check-in with yourself regularly and ask yourself if you are being the best version of you that you can. Do you still love the person that you are? If the answer is no, then something must change.

If you stop loving yourself, you might project these insecurities onto your friends. By making them feel unintentionally guilty for not building you up, it can be very easy to become a toxic friend that you would avoid yourself. Know that you can be just as happy alone as you can be with a friend. Hang out with yourself, and get to know yourself as you would another person. While these situations do not have to happen all the time, it is still a good idea to take part in them occasionally so that you know for sure that you still love yourself and the person that you are becoming.

Take the time to reinvent yourself, if you must. Do something new that you are unfamiliar with. When you have more friends, you will likely have more confidence. Know that you can still find ways to challenge yourself that will be different from the ways you utilized before. Put yourself in situations where you do not feel like you know exactly what is going to happen. This is a great way to catch yourself off guard and to really observe how you respond to new situations. You will probably find that there are many more interests that you may find yourself wanting to explore.

When you do not feel like yourself, open up to your friends. They might be able to remind you of the ways that you are truly a great person. It is common to lose sight of ourselves over time. This is something natural that nearly everyone must experience. It can happen a lot in socialization because of the pressure to transform into someone who is liked by the masses. Understand that not everyone has to like you. There is no obligation to please the world. As long as you are happy and you are treating your friends well, feel proud of who you are.

Chapter 9

Meeting People

Introducing Self and Other People

W hen people learn how to introduce themselves and others in informal and formal situations, their level of confidence tends to reach new heights. The skills of meeting people and making introductions are the foundation of bringing individuals together. People who have mastered these skills automatically and unconsciously play the role of host wherever they go, which can be quite interesting to watch.

People interact with several different social circles. Many socialize with workplace colleagues, neighbors, family members, and so on. In most cases, people keep their different social circles separate, either unintentionally or intentionally. However, there are many situations where those groups of people will meet, for example, at parties, funerals, weddings, and so on. When this happens, one may have to make numerous introductions.

Introducing Self

People are bound to see someone they do not know, no matter where they go. At a large get-together, party, or formal event, everyone should make the most of the opportunity by introducing self to others. A self-introduction to a new acquaintance is as easy as saying, "Hello, my name is (insert name here). I don't believe we've met." On the other hand, if the person one is approaching is familiar, using his or her name will make an individual's introduction a bit friendlier. For example, "Hi Mr. Simons, my name is ………………… It's an honor to meet you."

Introducing Others

If the people one is introducing are of the same gender and age range, it does not matter whose name one says first. However, if they are of different gender but are in the same age group, one should say the female's name first. For example, "Susan, this is my neighbor Paul. Paul, this is Susan." On the other hand, if they have a different age range, it is important to say the older an individual's name first. For example, "Uncle Simon, this is my friend, Ivy. Ivy, this is my uncle, Simon Books." Finally, if one of them is a VIP, his or her name should come first.

Things To Keep In Mind

It is important to remember that when introducing relatives, one should offer their full names. An individual's friends or co-workers would not call an individual's parents "Dad or Mom"; however, they might have to unless one tells them their names.

It is also helpful to add a little more information about that one is introducing. For example, Paul, this is Ivy. She loves hiking too." This gives Paul an excellent conversation starter and or topic, for which he will appreciate. In addition, a firm handshake and friendly smile will win everyone over and make a great impression.

Introducing Other Informal Settings

In work and other formal settings, it is important to use the first and last names when introducing individuals. Introductions made in formal settings, such as business events, should take rank and position into consideration. One should state the name of the most senior person first. For example, "Mr. Jackson (manager), this is our new Accountant, Samuel Sanders."

When introducing a special benefactor or client, state his or her name first. This applies even if the person to whom one is introducing him or her to has a higher position in an individual's place of work. For example, "Ivy Summers, please meet Professor Paul Strongman, who is our company's President." On the other hand, when introducing individuals of equal rank in the academic or corporate world, one should start with the person one knows less well.

Other Things To Keep In Mind

1. Following the introduction, always continue to address others as Mr. or Ms., unless one is expressly asked to use their first name. However, it is up to one whether to accept the offer or not.

2. It is important to use an individual's first and last name when introducing oneself.

3. At dinners or in formal settings, the host meets, greets, and introduces people who do not know each other. In networking events, however, people are free to introduce themselves.

4. Since some people tend to struggle when it comes to remembering names, re-introductions may be necessary.

It is important to make the most out of any introduction opportunity. Meeting a new person can be as fun as opening a gift. A new acquaintance may turn out to be a great client, best friend, or even an individual's future love. The benefits are endless. The only mistake one can make is not introducing self and other people when an opportunity arises.

Proper introductions help make people feel at ease in both formal and informal situations, which helps them have conversations more comfortable. In other words, the aim of introductions it to give people an opportunity to meet someone new. Knowing all the rules of introducing self and other people, as well as all types of introductions, should be easy for anyone. Mastering the skill of meeting people can help one look good to those whom one is meeting for the first time or introducing to others.

People Connections

People connection is simply the process of how human beings link up and form a deep understanding of each other when they realize they share the same goals and vision. People connections improve our social skills. This skill helps people avoid being anxious or awkward in social setups and instead put themselves out there.

Connecting with people nowadays can be either physically or by using technology. By just clicking a button, one can make new connections on different social platforms. However, the most important and valuable people connections happen face-to-face.

How Do You Meet New People?

In order to develop this skill, one has to meet new people first. The process of meeting new people can start by just talking to that co-worker you never say hello to or that neighbor you pass every day walking his dog. Attending things like art galleries, book clubs, cooking classes, or music recitals is a good way to meet new people. In order to meet new people, be open to trying out new things that you would otherwise say no to. When you establish the connections, show genuine interest.

How To Develop People Connection

Many of us struggle to meet people and develop connections with them. If one feels uncomfortable or shy about putting themselves out there, here are seven ways they can improve their people connection skills:

Being a social person - Many times, people avoid putting themselves in social situations that will make them feel shy, awkward, or anxious. In order to connect with others, talk, interact and mingle with people you do not know. Do not let shyness or anxiety hold you back.

Encourage them to talk about themselves - If one lacks this skill, the best way to start developing it is by encouraging others to talk about themselves in social setups. When conversing show interest in their careers, family or current events but avoid controversial topics like politics.

Offer flattering remarks - Learn to politely compliment or praise the people you meet on anything they have done or accomplished. If you are from watching them perform, commend them for their performance. This is usually an icebreaker when starting conversations.

Have proper etiquette - Politeness and good manners, in general, helps improve an individual's social skills. When approaching new people, ensure that you maintain proper etiquette, you actually do not know whom you will meet.

Have a target - Setting a target for yourself is a good way to develop this skill. If your target is to connect with two people per day, strive to talk to at least two people. You can start small then increase the target number when you get more confident.

Be keen on people's body language - One can learn a lot by just observing an individual's body language. Be keen to note if your presence is making someone comfortable or uncomfortable and react appropriately. Uncomfortable people will most likely not be open to holding a conversation for too long.

Pay attention - When meeting new people, it is always good to ensure that there are no distractions interrupting your conversations like a cell phone that keeps buzzing. Referring back to the things that they have just said shows you were actually listening and makes them want to listen to you even more.

How To Build On The Connections After The First Meeting

After connecting with people in social gatherings, the connection can quickly end as soon as the event is over. However, one can strengthen it by doing the following.

Extend an invitation - Once you establish common interests, be the one to break the ice and invite them for tea or to such-like events. Offer the invitation when winding up on the conversation. You will be surprised how many actually show up.

Exchange business cards - If it is a business setup, feel free to give out your business card, in case they want to get in touch with you and politely request for theirs.

Attend similar events - The best way to meet someone again after making that first connection is by attending another event similar to the one where you initially met. If you met at an art gallery, the chances of bumping into them in another art gallery are quite high.

The Benefit Of People Connections

Connecting with others and improving your social skills has the following benefits:

It boasts an individual's self-confidence - Being able to meet, interact, and connect with other people is a sure way of boosting an individual's self-confidence.

Helps build relationships - Making new connections can help build new relationships as well as future friendships. These new connections can open the door to new job opportunities or businesses, new friendships, and help you understand others better.

Improve communication - Connecting with others is likely to help one develop better communication skills. By connecting with many people, one is able to learn and grow their own communication skills.

Helps one become more efficient - By connecting with others, you quickly learn what you like and dislike about people and avoid people you do not like.

Not everyone in an event will be interested in connecting with you and vice versa. However, the goal is to focus on your targets and surpass them. Avoid dwelling on any rejections and celebrate any positive connections made.

Making Friends

Making friends is a social skill that everyone has to practice in their lifetime. When young, it was much easier to make friends than as an adult. This is true because kids are not afraid to show vulnerability. They do not dwell too much, into what they are ripping out of friendship as adults do. Friends become a big part of our lives. They are the people who will always be there through sad times and happy times. However, there are different types of friends:

1. Regular friends - One meets these friends every so often to catch up. Conversations with them are usually about regular topics

2. Acquaintances - These friends are the ones you meet every day just because you attend the same school or organization. Your conversation with them is usually hi-bye or how are you doing. You never meet them anywhere else.

3. Best friends - These are your ride or dies, and your conversations are not limited to anything. You trust each other and share very personal information. Even though you may not meet up often, your relationship is solid strong.

Most people strive to make regular as well as best friends.

Conditions For Making New Friends

The following are three conditions that allow people to make new friends:

1. Location- An individual's location and proximity can influence his or her ability to make new friends.

2. Repeat interactions- A person's openness to attending interactions like school or church can influence their ability to make friends

3. Open-mindedness- an individual's ability to put themselves out there can influence how often they connect with others

Tips For Making New Friends

Making friends can seem like an easy task, but a lot of people struggle with it. Here are a few pointers on how to make friends:

- Put yourself out there - In order to meet new people, and improve your social skills, be open to attending parties, workshops, clubs and any other social setups where people gather to do various activities. These gatherings offer a great way to meet people quickly.

- Make the first move - The same way you feel intimidated about approaching people you do not know is the same way others feel. Take the first step, say hello, and get to know the other person.

- Get to know people - Share something about yourself and give the other person an opportunity to share as well. Friendship is a two-way street. Start conversations about things that have happened recently.

- Have an open mind - People are diverse beings. You might be looking for friends who share common interests as you, and when you meet them, you end up not liking them. At the same time, you can meet people who are opposite and become best of friends.

- Be yourself - When meeting new people always be yourself. This helps them decide if they like the real you or not. Pretending to be someone else is hard work to maintain.

- Find a way to keep in touch - Making friends requires continual effort. Invite them out for lunch or tea or get their contacts and communicate every so often. Technology has made it possible to keep in touch.

- Stay up to date - A good way to break the ice is to start conversations about current events and news stories that everyone is talking about. Ask them what their take is on certain issues as long as they are not too controversial.

How To Keep Friends

Making friends is the easiest part; keeping them is usually the hard part.
Once you meet someone always:

1. Be real - Keeping it real is what builds a friendship. People
   appreciate friends who tell it like it is, friends who do not beat
   about the bush or lie in order to make them feel nice. Such
   friends are likely to reciprocate the same.

2. Be present - In order to keep long-lasting friendships, being
   present in each other's life is important. This does not only mean
   being physically there but also connecting with them either
   through text messages, calls, or on social platforms.

3. Be understanding - As much as friendship is a two-way street,
   sometimes life happens and one cannot show up for all the
   birthday parties and hangouts. Instead of assuming, they do not
   care, be understanding, and reach out to them. You never know
   what someone is going through.

Importance Of Making Friends

Making Friends comes with many benefits. Your friends are the people
who will be with you through the difficulties of life, challenge us to grow
and at the same time, drive us nuts; however, they are important for our
well-being.

1. Friends help us improve our social skills - By putting yourself out
   there to meet and make new friends; you are improving your

social skills. Meeting people requires communicating and interacting with others.

2. Friends are important to our health - Friends are equally important as the food we eat. We need them to keep us physically and mentally strong and healthy.

3. Friends improve our quality of life - Despite what life throws at us, friends help us improve our quality of life. Friends will always be there to laugh, cry, support, help us, and put things into perspective.

4. Friends improve our relationships with others - Through friends, we can meet and interact with new people. Many of our relationships with others are based on friendships.

Bottom line, you need friends, and they need you. Meeting people is an important social skill that is necessary. Finding, picking and keeping the right friends will always be part of our lives.

Making Use Of Social Media

In 2019, there are 3.4 billion social media users throughout the world, and with technology advancing more and more people are connecting online. The beauty of it is that people are able to travel across the world and still keep in touch. Social media has opened up new doors for people to improve their social skills; however now individuals need to keep up with the new applications and the ever-evolving tech world.

While social media does not offer the deep connections that come with connecting with people face-to-face, it offers more convenience. It has greatly challenged our social skills but also provided endless ways for people to connect online.

Advantages Of Social Media

1. People can stay connected - Social media has enabled people to keep in touch

2. Job opportunities - Many people are earning a living through various social media platforms.

3. Networking - It is easy for people to meet and make connections.

4. Support - People online can be compassionate, especially when it comes to supporting a cause, seeking justice or support people going through difficult times.

5. Marketing - Many businesses now use social media for marketing their products and services.

6. Enhance Education - Students all over the world can take courses online. They can receive assignments and participate in discussions using various social media platforms.

Disadvantages Of Social Media

Just like most good things, social media also has a negative side to it. A few disadvantages include:

1. Cyberbullying- Social media has created ab opportunity for people to send messages to threaten and intimidate others.

2. Challenge our social skills - These platforms have made people so glued to technology that they struggle holding a normal conversation with people physically.

3. Create false assumptions - People only share what they want you to see and not their real lives.

4. Comparing our own lives to other people - People sometimes fall into the trap of comparing themselves to others, forgetting that people only share what they want you to see.

5. The internet always remembers - It is very difficult to delete something once shared on the internet, and sometimes things have a way of coming back to haunt you.

6. Low productivity - People can spend hours perusing through social media, instead of doing other constructive things. It is more or less an addiction.

Importance Of Social Media

1. Boosting people's confidence - When people share their photos and videos, they get a lot of feedback from others, which in turn can motivate them to share more things that get them out of their comfort zone.

2. Getting news in real-time - With headlines appearing at our fingertips, social media keeps people up to date on current trends and news.

3. Improve lifestyle change - Many people, such as celebrities; promote their healthy lifestyle through these platforms. They

share exercise routines, diets, and products that they use to motivate their followers to make the change.

4. Freedom of speech - with the various platforms, social media has made it possible for people to express themselves.

5. Help people to reconnect - Many people have reconnected with their old friends through social media. It actually made things easy when trying to track someone down.

How to Make Use of Social Media to Improve Our Social Skills

Using social media platforms can be seen as a big waste of time, but this is not the case. These platforms can help one reach millions of people all over the world in a split second. In order to improve our social skills online we can:

1. Creating videos - Social media platforms usually allow their users to share photos, video, or texts with other people. In order to improve our social skills, one can opt to share content using a video as opposed to writing or texting. Videos give a clearer view of what one is trying to communicate.

2. Offer good customer care - People online use the various social media platforms to rant, complain, and share their disappointments about a product or service they disliked. Companies and businesses in question can use the same platforms to listen to their customers and address their concerns.

3. Identify the target market - One can use social media to reach a certain target market. These platforms offer the ability to share posts to a specific area in order to reach your target audience.

4. Staying Active - Engaging and interacting with people online at all times is one way of improving an individual's social skills. In addition, being consistent helps build on old connections as well as gain new ones.

5. Broke Barriers - Social media has broken down barriers of communicating with others. We can now keep in contact with anyone directly as long as he or she is also using the same platforms.

Social media platforms have greatly improved our communication skills, what we can do, is using to them improve our own social skills and life in general. These platforms will only become more pervasive in our lives, so the sooner we get on the bandwagon, the better.

Conclusion

I
f you desire to enjoy all that life has to offer, improving your social skills is non negotiable. It is high time you crawl out of the shell you have built for yourself due to social anxiety, shyness, and lack of confidence. Remaining in this shell will only end up robbing you of all the goodness and riches out there. There is meaning and sense in life when enjoyed in the company of others, and not in isolation.

If there is one thing I regret about my early years, it is not working on developing my social skills. When I think about how awesome my life could have been, the opportunities and relationships that I missed out on makes me sad. And I am sure there are many people in my shoes. Luckily, I was able to take practical steps to improve and get my social life in order before I become and old man full of regrets.

You can also do the same. It is not too late to develop charisma and initiate contact with that girl you have always eyed. You have potential; do not let shyness and lack of confidence rob you of maximizing your potentials to the fullest. In my quest to improve my social skills, one of the things that got me going is that people are too busy with their lives to capitalize on how I made a fool of myself. They are actually interested in what I have to say than how I comport myself. Armed with this information, launching out was easy for me.

The practice and tips presented in this manual will not transform you overnight. Besides, it is not about theoretical knowledge alone. You have to get out there. We have presented tons of information in this manual. Be sure to take each chapter and work on the recommended ideas and suggestions. With time, dedication, and resilience, you will notice considerable improvement. Rome was not built in a day, they say. And as with any other skill, social skills takes time and effort. It is a course on its own. Besides, looking at the amazing turnaround that developing your social skills can have on your life, it is worth every effort.

I am pretty sure if you can pay the price to work on developing your social skills, your future self will thank you. It will not come on a platter of gold. Your voice might fail you at times. You might sweat and even forget what you wanted to say. Do not beat yourself up. Whether you see it or not, your efforts are all working together to help build your social muscles.

Remember, baby steps. By getting yourself out there, you have overcome the greatest barrier. And by keeping up with the practice, you condition yourself for improved social skills. It is also important that I point out that you will face rejection. I do not mean to be a prophet of doom, but to prepare your mind. When you are rejected, do not take that as an excuse to recoil into your shell. Let the rejection be a fuel to help you bounce back and also get better at handling rejection. Bear in mind that everyone who succeeded has failure as part of their success story.

Building your social skill is not rocket science. I am pretty sure there are many people out there that were once socially awkward. These people, however, got uncomfortable with their life and took the necessary steps. These are people who, when you see them today, you wish you were like them. You might, however, not realize something – they paid the price. You can as well. And with utmost dedication, you can improve your social skills such that it becomes a natural part of you.

CPSIA information can be obtained
at www.ICGtesting.com
Printed in the USA
LVHW081919010621
689024LV00016B/1502